EXPERT SECRETS

"Expert Secrets is the map that will allow you to turn your specialized knowledge, talents, and abilities into a business that will work for you! This is one of the shortcuts of the new rich."
—Robert Kiyosaki

EXPERT
SECRETS
THE UNDERGROUND PLAYBOOK
TO FIND YOUR MESSAGE, BUILD A TRIBE,
AND CHANGE THE WORLD...
RUSSELL BRUNSON

NEW YORK

NASHVILLE • MELBOURNE • VANCOUVER

EXPERT SECRETS
THE UNDERGROUND PLAYBOOK TO FIND YOUR MESSAGE, BUILD A TRIBE, AND CHANGE THE WORLD...

© 2017 **RUSSELL BRUNSON**

Published in New York, New York, by Morgan James Publishing. Morgan James is a trademark of Morgan James, LLC. www.MorganJamesPublishing.com

The Morgan James Speakers Group can bring authors to your live event. For more information or to book an event visit The Morgan James Speakers Group at www.TheMorganJamesSpeakersGroup.com.

ISBN 978-1-68350-458-0 paperback
ISBN 978-1-68350-459-7 eBook
Library of Congress Control Number: 2017902207

Cover Design: Rob Secades
Illustrations by: Vlad Babich
Cover Photography: Dan Usher

In an effort to support local communities, raise awareness and funds, Morgan James Publishing donates a percentage of all book sales for the life of each book to Habitat for Humanity Peninsula and Greater Williamsburg.

Get involved today! Visit
www.MorganJamesBuilds.com

DEDICATION

To Deagan Smith, who reignited my passion for marketing during a dark time in my journey, when I almost threw in the towel. I'm so grateful that your inspiration gave me a second chance.

To the experts I've met in my life who helped me to become who I am today. Many of you have had a huge impact on my life in wrestling, religion, business, health, and my relationships. Thanks for being willing to contribute so I could grow.

And to my amazing kids, Dallin, Bowen, Ellie, Aiden, and Norah, who have given me a reason to try to make this world a better place. Your future is what drives me today.

CONTENTS

FOREWORD

"Expert Secrets **is the map that will allow you to turn your specialized knowledge, talents, and abilities into a business that will work for you! This is one of the shortcuts of the new rich."**
by Robert Kiyosaki

You have something special inside you. Something you know. Something you do. Something you can teach. You are already an expert. We all have this something special inside of us and, if we use it right, we can change the world—and become rich in the process.

Information is a powerful tool. It can be used to attract interest, increase desire, demand attention, and sell. But information alone isn't enough. It's the skillful application of the right information at the right time that can change your life.

If you aren't familiar with my work, I teach a system called the Cashflow Quadrant. I explain that you are in one of four places in

CASHFLOW QUADRANT

Employee	Business Owner
E	**B**
S	**I**
Self Employed	Investor

your work life. You're either an employee (E), you're self-employed (S), you own a business (B), or you're an investor (I). Most of us start out as E, and some never leave this stage. To become financially free, though, you must move through the quadrants and get to the business and investor stages as quickly as possible.

Information is how that's done. Information that's already inside you. Think about it. What do you know? What can you teach others?

My Rich Dad Company is essentially an expert business. I offer financial education through a variety of products, programs, courses, and mentorships. It started with *CASHFLOW*, a simple game that transforms lives with the lessons it teaches. Then we expanded into lectures and books and coaching platforms. My information business grew organically. I didn't have a step-by-step plan. Thanks to this book, you do.

In *Expert Secrets*, Russell Brunson has masterfully laid out the steps to becoming a thought leader and building a following of people who will pay you for your information. You can literally start from zero and by the end you will have your own profitable business. He gives you the concepts, the scripts, the technology—everything. And by the time you finish this book, you will naturally be in the third quadrant. You will be a business owner.

Russell has compiled decades of study and distilled the process down so you can succeed no matter where you're starting from. And you can do it all based on what you already know, even if you don't feel confident just yet.

As Russell explains in this book, "regular" businesses can use the Expert Secrets process to create and sell information, too. Doctors, dentists, professional services, and even retail stores can all use what they know to create useful information that attracts customers. In fact, if you attach an information business to the front end of your existing business, you can reduce your customer acquisition costs to practically zero (and even get paid for every new customer that enters your world).

If you're an employee, you can use the Expert Secrets process to set up your own business quickly.

If you're self-employed or run a small business, you can use the Expert Secrets process to grow that company.

And because expert businesses are some of the most profitable businesses in the world, you'll be able to take the profits from your company and become an investor. That is how you build true wealth.

You'll read case studies in this book that show how real people just like you have moved through the quadrants at incredible speed. In fact, you might just skip a quadrant or two.

In the past, there were incredible technical and financial hurdles that had to be overcome in order to move through the quadrants. If you were an employee and wanted to start your own business on the side, you either hired a web designer or learned how to do it yourself. You either hired a copywriter or learned how to do it yourself. You either hired someone to run your shopping cart or learned how to do it yourself, all of which was expensive and time-consuming.

But when you use this book with ClickFunnels (a software tool Russell created that we use in the Rich Dad organization), you'll have all the tools you need to handle the complex technical aspects of running an expert business as well! You don't need to pay tens of thousands of dollars to designers and coders anymore. The financial and technical barriers have been removed so you can focus on sharing your message with the world.

People often ask me, "What does it take to make money?" My answer is that it takes a dream, a lot of determination, a willingness to learn quickly, and the ability to use your God-given assets properly.

Then they ask, "How do you do that? What's the path?"

Expert Secrets is the path. You hold in your hand the step-by-step roadmap to turning those assets into wealth and prosperity.

Learn.

Take action.

And enjoy the ride.

Robert T. Kiyosaki

ACKNOWLEDGMENTS

I wanted to start by giving a very special thanks to Daegan Smith. A few years back, he had a conversation with me about "belief" and what's possible when someone truly believes in something. We then started talking about how we could create that true belief in the minds of the people we were trying to serve. That one conversation took me on a journey that lasted over five years and has resulted in this book. You will see many things I learned that day and over the next few years from Daegan woven into these pages. Without his ideas, this book wouldn't have been possible.

I want to thank Perry Belcher, for helping me understand new opportunities and status, Dan Kennedy for teaching me how to use character and communication, Michael Hauge for showing me story structure, Blair Warren for his work with persuasion, Jason Fladlien for teaching me how to break and rebuild belief patterns, and Armand Morin for creating the stack. Those concepts created the foundation this book was built on.

I'm so grateful for my Inner Circle members and people inside of our "Funnel Hacker" community, who are willing to take these crazy ideas and test them in literally hundreds of different markets. You've given us the ability to test things at scale in a way that has never been possible in the history of direct response marketing. We're able to see what things work in which markets, and make adjustments based on that feedback. This book is infinitely better because of your real-world, in-the-trenches testing of these concepts.

I also know that none of this would be possible if it weren't for my team here at ClickFunnels—Todd Dickerson, Dylan Jones, Ryan Montgomery and the rest of the development team—for building ClickFunnels and continuing to make it better every day. This platform is what has given entrepreneurs like me the ability to get our messages out to the world. John Parkes, Dave Woodward, and the rest of our marketing team for helping us to get ClickFunnels and this message into the hands of every entrepreneur in the world. Brent Coppieters and his support team for creating the best possible customer experience for our entrepreneurs. And everyone else who is helping to serve our community. There are so many amazing people who are part of the movement we are creating here at ClickFunnels, it would be impossible to name them all.

And last, I want to thank Stephen Larsen, for being a constant sounding board during this book project. Without your excitement for this book, it never would have been completed. And Julie Eason, for dedicating the better part of a year to help me write this book…twice. If it weren't for you, this would still just be a bunch of random thoughts inside my head.

Thank you.

WHAT IS EXPERT SECRETS?

Expert Secrets is the second half of a journey you have already started. Something you experienced in your life started you on this path, which caused you to want to become more. You started to read books, study, and experiment with the things you learned, and by doing so you have become who you are today, an EXPERT.

But as most experts soon find, no matter how much personal development you achieve, there will be a point where you can no longer progress. The only way to continue to grow is by helping others become like you. Yes, true growth and fulfillment comes from your contribution to others.

Your message has the ability to change someone's life. The impact that the right message can have on someone at the right time in their life is immeasurable. It could help to save marriages, repair families, change someone's health, grow a company or more...

But only if you know how to get it into the hands of the people whose lives you have been called to change.

Expert Secrets will help you find your voice and give you the confidence to become a leader...

Expert Secrets will show you how to build a mass movement of people whose lives you can affect...

Expert Secrets will teach you how to make this calling a career, where people will pay you for your advice...

As Sir Winston Churchill once said:

To each there comes in their lifetime a special moment when they are figuratively tapped on the shoulder and offered the chance to do a very special thing, unique to them and fitted to their talents. What a tragedy if that moment finds them unprepared or unqualified for that which could have been their finest hour.

Your message matters, and this book is your figurative tap on the shoulder.

INTRODUCTION

I had just gotten married earlier that year, which meant I was one of just two married guys on the Boise State wrestling team. It was spring break and all of our friends had jumped into their cars to make the six-hour drive to Vegas to celebrate. But Nathan Ploehn and I were stuck at home because the beautiful women we had married earlier were working hard to support their jobless, wrestling husbands.

I was a sophomore at Boise State University. For months leading up to spring break, I had been studying marketing and learning how to sell things online. At that point, almost everything I tried failed. I tried selling on eBay and made a little bit of money, but not enough to cover the shipping and listing fees. I tried selling things on Craigslist. I tried becoming an affiliate.

Nothing seemed to work, and I was a little desperate to figure out something that actually made good money. It's funny looking back now. I didn't set out to become a potato gun expert, but that's exactly what happened.

On the third day of spring break, after we'd watched about a dozen movies, we decided we had to get out of the house and do something. That's when Nate said, "Hey, we should make a potato gun."

I had heard of potato guns before, but I'd never actually seen one. He told me how you could make them by gluing PVC pipes together. When they're dry, you jam a potato down the barrel, spray hairspray into the chamber, create a little spark, and shoot them a few hundred yards! I was so excited I could barely contain myself!

There was only one problem—we didn't know how to make one.

So we found some websites that had free potato gun plans. During our research, we found out a bunch of interesting things. We learned you had to have the correct barrel-to-chamber volume ratio or your potatoes wouldn't shoot very far. We found out the right propellant to use, the correct pressure for the pipes, and lots of other important details. We also learned how to keep ourselves safe (meaning which kinds of pipes and propellants would blow up and which ones wouldn't). It didn't take long before we knew a ton of great information about potato guns.

Armed with this information, we were ready to make our first gun. So we went to Home Depot and bought the pipes, glue, barbeque

POTATO GUN EXPERT

$$\pi r 2 * L$$

Barrel To Chamber Ratio

Potatoes

igniters, and other things we needed. We spent the next few days making the gun and, when it was finished, we found a secluded location and started shooting it. We had one of the best times of our lives. It was so much fun!

We spent the rest of that week making more guns, trying out other plans, and even creating some designs of our own. During that week, we learned more about potato guns than 95% of the world would ever know. In fact, you might say we became experts.

The next Monday when school started back up again, I remember sitting in a finance class wishing I was out shooting potato guns, and I had a flash of inspiration. I thought, *I wonder if anyone else besides me searched for information on how to make potato gun plans last weekend.* There are places online where you can see how many searches in Google are happening each month. So I went to one of those websites, typed in the keywords "potato gun", and found that over 18,000 people that month had searched for the phrase "potato gun plans"!

At that time, there were no products, no plans, and no other experts out there teaching people about potato guns. There was a lot of free stuff, but nothing for sale. It occurred to me that this was my chance. This was my opportunity to become an expert in potato guns, and to sell my advice. I figured I knew about as much as any other "potato gun expert" out there, so all I needed to do was create a product and sell it. I called Nate and convinced him to help me record a demo of us making potato guns. We borrowed a little video camera and drove up to Home Depot.

When we got there and started filming, someone asked us what we were doing. We told them we were recording a video about making potato guns. Apparently, Home Depot didn't want that type of liability, and they threw us out. So we drove to the next Home Depot in town, and this time we went into stealth mode. I hid the camera under my jacket, then pulled it out and started recording what we were buying as we bought the pipes, barbecue igniters, and propellants.

We returned home and filmed ourselves assembling the guns. We described each step as we did it, shared the secret barrel-to-chamber volume ratios we'd discovered, told them about our favorite propellants, and instructed them how to keep safe. Eventually, we had a video explaining the whole process. Then we turned our homemade video into a DVD to sell online.

While I never became a millionaire as a potato gun expert, we did make sales. In fact, we averaged anywhere from $20 to $30 a day selling that product, which was huge for a couple of college kids. It completely transformed my life and helped me understand the power of an expert business.

Now as inspiring as selling potato gun DVDs can be, I believe the true value of an expert business isn't the money you make, but the people's lives you're able to change through your message. And while the people who bought my DVDs were able to have a great time making potato guns, I felt like what I had learned from the process of selling my first information product was just a stepping-stone for something bigger. Something I was meant to do. Little did I know at that time that this was where my real journey would begin. A journey that has lasted over a decade now.

I started to find other experts in areas of life that fascinated me. We took their messages and promoted them through this Expert Secrets system I was developing. Many of the early projects we worked on failed. But with each failure came a lesson on what worked and, more importantly, what didn't work. I became obsessed with why people buy and what you can do to influence their purchasing decisions.

Even more rewarding was the impact that the right message can have on someone at the right time in their life. Like when someone is trying to lose weight, and they find an expert who resonates with them, inspires them, and gives them the right opportunity to finally make that change. Or the person who is trying to do better in school, or a couple trying to strengthen their marriage, or an entrepreneur who wants to grow a company—we all need help to grow. And we seek out experts for that help.

One of our companies helps people overcome pornography addiction. We partnered with an expert, created an information product, and started selling it online. Our message landed in the hands of men who were struggling with this addiction. Wives and mothers found our courses and used them to better understand the people they love who struggled with this addiction. We started to make money but, more importantly, we watched as marriages were saved, families were repaired, and people's lives were changed forever. That's real impact. That's powerful.

THAT is what this book is about.

Yes—if you follow the system, then you will make money. But that is not the point, that is merely the by-product of helping others. Zig Ziglar once said: "You will get all you want in life, if you help enough other people get what they want."

THE TWO TYPES OF EXPERT BUSINESSES

Before we get too deep, I want to point out that there are two types of expert businesses. The tactics behind both are the same, but the strategies are a little different. Let me explain each of them so you can see which one best fits what you are trying to create.

EXPERT BUSINESS #1: SELLING INFORMATION PRODUCTS

The first type of expert business is the one that most of you will probably be creating. It involves you taking the life lessons that you've learned, and packaging them into information products, coaching, and consulting. Being an expert and selling information products is (in my opinion) the greatest start-up in the world. You don't need venture or start-up capital, just a passion for what you're teaching, as well as learning how to tell stories in a way that will get others excited about it as well.

I have hundreds of fun stories I could tell you about people who have taken their talents, ideas, and unique abilities to grow expert-

Expert Business #1
Selling Information Products

based companies. One of my favorite stories is from one of my friends, Jacob Hiller.

Growing up, Jacob always wanted to be able to dunk a basketball but, for whatever reasons, he wasn't able to. It bothered him so much that he made it a mission to figure out how to increase his vertical jump. He researched all sorts of different regimens and became a human guinea pig, testing these ideas out one by one. As he started having success, he would record videos showing the techniques that worked and post them on a YouTube channel he created.

At first, nobody really cared. But he was focusing on himself and improving his own vertical jump, so it didn't matter. He recorded the videos for free and put them online because he loved it. Over time, people started noticing. They started to share his message with their friends, and soon he built this nice little following of people just like him who were interested in learning how to jump higher.

He went from having 0 followers to 100...then 1,000...and 10,000...and beyond, just by sharing what he was passionate about. This is how many expert businesses start. You find something you're passionate about, and your obsession with learning and applying helps you become an expert who can lead others. His viewers kept asking for more, and that's when he realized he'd built something incredibly unique. He then started creating products to teach others what he had learned and turned it into a company that now makes millions of dollars teaching people how to jump.

As cool as Jacob's story is, it's not unique. Another one of my friends, Jermaine Griggs, struggled with reading sheet music and became great at playing piano by ear. He now makes millions a year from helping others learn how to play piano by ear. My student Liz Benny was an amazing social media manager for herself and others, but when she became an expert and started teaching others how to do it, she made millions.

Robert G. Allen, the great real estate investor and coach, once said that he made millions DOING real estate, but he made hundreds of millions TEACHING it.

That's how it typically starts. We get excited about a topic and we start geeking out on it. We learn, we read books, we study examples, we listen to podcasts, and we consume a lot of information. Then we start using it for ourselves. At some point, we realize the only way to keep growing isn't to learn more, but instead to shift our focus from personal growth to contribution. It's only by shifting our focus to helping others that we continue to grow. We coach others, we create information products, and we start contributing to other people's growth. When you do that, you learn more about yourself and the process as you do it.

Contribution is the key to continued growth.

The first time I truly understood that, I was in high school. I was a state champion and an all-American wrestler. I read and watched everything I could about wrestling. My dad and I would study videos and practice moves every day.

Then the summer after my senior year, one of my coaches asked me if I'd help coach at the wrestling camp. I'd never coached wrestling before, but thought it would be fun. When I started, I was coaching the younger wrestlers on moves I was intuitively good at, but that others couldn't figure out. At first it was really difficult to break down and explain why the move worked and how they were supposed to do it. But as I taught the kids, I started to notice why the move wasn't working for them. And I'd say, "It's not working because your arm is bent the wrong way." Or "You're at the wrong angle." By teaching, I had to dissect what I was doing and learn WHY it worked.

As I became aware of those details, I was able to better teach them to the kids. And the awareness I gained from coaching also made me a much better athlete. Contributing to other people's success helped me grow more than focusing on my own success.

The process with most expert businesses is the same. First, we become passionate about a particular topic. We study, we learn, we implement, but eventually we can't grow anymore from study alone. We then shift our focus to helping others with what we have learned, and that contribution helps them, which in turn also helps us continue to grow.

EXPERT BUSINESS #2: LEVERAGING INFORMATION PRODUCTS TO GROW AN EXISTING COMPANY

If you already have a company, you can use this Expert Secrets system to quickly grow your company and get customers for free. I was hesitant to title this book "Expert Secrets", because I didn't want people to dismiss it simply because they sell other types of products or services besides information.

Many people ask me how we turned ClickFunnels into the fastest growing SAAS (software as a service) company in the history of the internet without venture capital or any kind of start-up backing. The answer is that I first focused on selling information products as an expert

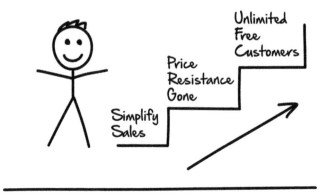

Expert Business #2
Leveraging Info Products As Fuel

that indoctrinated our customers, and made them desire the real service we were trying to sell them.

Our competitors and venture capitalists who have tried to invest with us couldn't understand how our cost to acquire a customer was better than free. As you'll soon see, each of our customers purchases an information product from us to start, and we actually make money on that first transaction. Later, we introduce those customers to ClickFunnels, making our cost to acquire a customer less than $0—because we already got paid when they purchased our information products!

We're actually getting paid to acquire customers, which gives us the ability to acquire tens of thousands of customers, almost overnight without spending any money out of our pockets.

When you start using the Expert Secrets process for your company, you'll find that a few amazing things will happen.

1. Complicated sales will become easy because the information products will indoctrinate potential customers about WHY they need your product or service.

2. You will be positioned as an expert instead of a commodity, and people will pay you MORE for the same thing they could get somewhere else. All other options will become irrelevant, price resistance will disappear, and future sales will become easier.
3. You will be able to acquire unlimited customers for free, so every backend sale you make will result in 100% profit.
4. You'll be able to grow MUCH faster.

This book has taken me over a decade to "earn" through trial and error, making thousands of offers to millions of people. I am only sharing strategies and tactics with you that are proven to work.

I hope you enjoy this book and that it will help amplify your message to the world.

CREATING YOUR MASS MOVEMENT

CREATING A MASS MOVEMENT

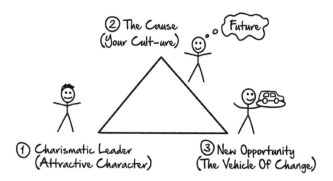

Before we get started, I need to share something that might seem a little backward at first, but it is one of the keys to sharing and monetizing your message. As you know, the world is filled with experts who are broke, people with advice and opinions and no one listening to them.

When I first started on this journey, I realized that if I was going to have success, I needed to focus first on building an audience of people I could share my message with. I wasn't sure where to go or how to do that. So I started studying historical figures who had built huge audiences and caused big changes. The more examples I found, the more patterns I noticed.

It didn't matter if I was studying Adolph Hitler and the Nazi party or Jesus Christ and Christianity; all the examples I found had three things in common that helped them build a mass movement.

1. They each had a charismatic leader or an attractive character.
2. Each of them focused on a future-based cause that was bigger than themselves.
3. They each offered their audience a new opportunity.

After noticing this pattern, I dug deeper into each of those three things to reverse engineer what was happening, and figure out why it worked. What I discovered was fascinating, and once I felt like I understood what worked, my team and I applied those principles to my audience. And I watched as people quickly transformed from mere followers into true fans.

In 2008, Kevin Kelly wrote an article called "1,000 True Fans". In that article, he said:

A creator, such as an artist, musician, photographer, craftsperson, performer, animator, designer, videomaker, or author—in other words, anyone producing works of art—needs to acquire only 1,000 True Fans to make a living.

A True Fan is defined as someone who will purchase anything and everything you produce. They will drive 200 miles to see you sing. They will buy the super deluxe re-issued hi-res box set of your stuff even though they have the low-res version. They have a Google Alert set for your name. They bookmark the eBay page where your out-of-print editions show up. They come to your openings. They have you sign their copies. They buy the t-shirt, and the mug, and the hat. They can't wait till you issue your next work. They are true fans.

This section is all about HOW to create those true fans, how to build your following. We have a joke inside my highest-level mastermind group (called the Inner Circle) that each of them must focus on building their own CULT-ures. While we're not actually building a cult, we are consciously creating a culture of true fans. And this section will show you how to do the same so you can create a vehicle for change in your fans' lives.

THE CHARISMATIC LEADER / ATTRACTIVE CHARACTER

Charismatic Leader /
Attractive Character

E very great mass movement has a leader. It's easy to assume that some people are just born leaders and others are not. It's possible that your biggest fear when you first read the title *Expert Secrets* was that you aren't a born leader or an expert. I know that was true for me, and still is some of the time.

In my personal life, I am pretty shy and reserved. But when I'm in my element, speaking about the topics that I've mastered, I am able to lead. You see, people become leaders when they first try to master something for themselves. Then after they've discovered a path for themselves, they share their knowledge with others. It starts with your own personal growth, but then transitions to contribution.

GROWTH → CONTRIBUTION

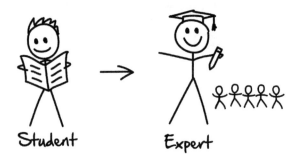

So if you're nervous about having what it takes to be a charismatic leader, I want to spend a few minutes talking to you. My guess is that you are amazing. And I bet that the more amazing you are, the harder it is for you to believe it. Am I right?

I've had a really rare opportunity to coach thousands of experts around the world in almost every market you can dream of. What's interesting is when I look at all these amazing people changing the lives of tens of thousands (and in some cases millions) of people, almost all of them have felt an internal pull to want to serve and help people. It's almost like a voice inside them telling them they are destined for greatness.

Yet at the same time, they have this other voice that consistently tells them they're inadequate, that they're not enough. Not smart enough, not focused enough, not thin enough, not experienced enough, not good enough...

The strange thing is that often the more they do and the more people they help, the louder the voice of inadequacy becomes. Whether you're just starting this journey or you've been at it for a while, just know that the biggest hurdle you're likely to face is being okay with positioning yourself as an expert.

What's equally important to understand is you're not alone. I really feel for people struggling with that negative inner voice because, in all honesty, that's the way I often feel. I feel like I have been blessed beyond what any human being should ever be blessed with on this Earth. And I feel that this gift I've been given from God is something I must share. In fact, if I don't share it, that would be an injustice to Him and the people I could serve.

Yet as I am out there in the trenches every single day building companies, working with entrepreneurs, trying to change the world in my own little way, I still wrestle with these feelings of inadequacy. As I talk to people, I realize that these same feelings keep most people from ever taking on the mantle of an expert. The voice keeps them from stepping up and stepping into that role.

And it's a tragedy for a couple of reasons. First, it deprives them of the experience and the opportunities they should have. And more importantly, it deprives the people whose lives they could change. Those people you could serve by sharing your God-given talents and expert abilities—they might never be reached.

So I want to pause here and take a moment, not so much to convince you that you're an expert, but to give you whatever permission you might need to be able to move forward. You have the ability—and, I believe, the responsibility—to serve others with your gifts, whatever they are.

You've been blessed with talents, ideas, and unique abilities that have gotten you to where you are in life, and those gifts were given to you so you could share them with others. There are people today who need what you have. And they are just waiting for you to find your voice, so you can help them change their lives. What a tragedy for them if you don't develop your voice now.

The problem for most of us is that our unique abilities are things that come second nature to us. So they don't seem that amazing, and we dismiss them.

For example, I would say that one of my superpowers is being able to look at a business or a product line and within seconds know exactly how the owner should be selling those products. I know what the scripts need to say. I know what the sales process needs to be. All these things just come so clearly to me. As soon as I see a product, I just know. For whatever reason, that's my unique superpower.

Now I wasn't born with this power. I've spent over a decade of my life studying this stuff, learning and experimenting with it. I've immersed myself in it for so long that now I can just instantly see what needs to happen. To me, it seems like common sense. How can people NOT see what I see? I might dismiss that skill because it comes so easily to me. But to other people, what I have is a superpower. It's a gift. And it's a skill that people will pay hundreds of thousands of dollars to learn from me. Not because I'm great, but because I've spent so much time mastering this one skill.

My guess is that your superpower won't seem like that big of a deal to you either. It will be something that comes second nature— something so simple that it couldn't possibly be that important. If you're an amazing cook, it's not that big of a deal for you. But to someone who can't cook, it's a HUGE deal.

Maybe you're good at playing piano, fixing motorcycles, building chicken coops, dancing, or something else. Look at what comes easy to you and what you love to geek out on, and chances are that's where your superpower is hiding, just waiting to be developed and shared with the world.

"But Russell, I'm not certified. I can't help people yet." This is one objection I hear WAY too often. "I'm not certified. I don't have a degree. I haven't been to school for this. How can I possibly claim to be an expert?" I always smile when I hear these words come out of someone's mouth because I know where I came from.

I ask them, "Well, I'm curious. You paid me $25,000 (or $100,000) to teach you this stuff. What do you think my credentials are?"

They think about it and usually say something like, "I don't know. Do you have any marketing degrees?"

I say, "Nope. I barely graduated from college, and I got a C in marketing." I didn't get good grades, and I don't have any certifications to my name. But guess what? I'm REALLY GOOD at what I do. My results are my certifications.

Tony Robbins told me that when he first started learning neuro-linguistic programming (NLP), he signed up for a six-month training course, and after just a few days, he fell in love with it. He gained skill quickly and wanted to start helping people immediately. The trainers said, "You can't, you're not certified yet."

Tony said, "Certified? I know how to help people. Let's go help!" That night, he left his hotel room, walked across the street to the nearest restaurant, and started helping people quit smoking and assisting them with lots of other amazing things. He ended up getting kicked out of the program because he was practicing without being certified. Yet he's gone on to transform tens of millions of people's lives using NLP—all without any certifications.

Your results are your certification.

I hereby give you permission to help people. You're ready now.

"But Russell, what if others know more about my topic than me?" There's a book (and a movie) called *Catch Me If You Can* that illustrates this point pretty well. It's the story of a famous con artist, Frank Abagnale, a brilliant high school dropout who masqueraded as an airline pilot, a pediatrician, and a district attorney, among other things.

There is a point in the book where he starts teaching a sociology class at Brigham Young University. He teaches the whole semester, and no one ever figures out that he's not a real teacher. Later on when they finally do catch him, the authorities ask, "How in the world did you teach that class? You don't know anything about advanced sociology."

He replied, "All I had to do was read one chapter ahead of the students."

That's the key. You don't have to be the most knowledgeable person in the world on your topic, you just have to be one chapter ahead of the people you're helping. There will always be people in the world who are more advanced than you. That's fine. You can learn from them, but don't let it stop you from helping the ones who are a chapter or two behind you.

WHO DO YOU WANT TO SERVE?

If you're going to start a mass movement and create a vehicle for change, the first question you have to ask yourself is "WHO do I want to serve?" The answer to that question is typically people who were just like you before you became an expert, right? As a charismatic leader, you're going to lead people on a path you've walked before.

Sometimes it can be hard to identify exactly who those people are. If you look closely, you'll find that almost all expert businesses are based on one of three core markets: health, wealth, or relationships. So my first question for you is which of those three matches your area of expertise right now?

THE 3 MARKETS

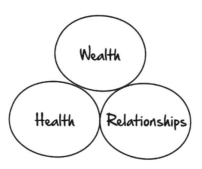

Ok, now that you've identified which core market you fit into, we need to dig at least two levels deep to find your specific audience. Let me show you what I mean.

THE 3 MARKETS

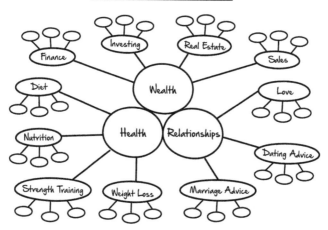

Inside these three core markets are multiple submarkets. For example, inside health you could have dozens of submarkets like diet, nutrition, strength training, and weight loss. Inside the wealth market you may have finance, investing, real estate, and sales. And the same goes for the relationships market. You could have love, dating advice, marriage, and parenting. The list is practically endless in any of the three core markets. There are always new submarkets popping up.

My next question for you is what submarket does your area of expertise fit right now? Some of you may think that you've found your answer. You're a real estate expert, or a dating or weight loss coach. But the money is NOT in the submarket. The riches are in the niches. And those are one step beyond the submarket.

Look around at the other experts in your submarket and see what they are selling. Where do you fit into the ecosystem? What can you offer people that's different and special? The goal is to carve out a unique spot in that ecosystem where you can thrive. That's your niche. And that niche is one of the keys to success as an expert.

In the book *Blue Ocean Strategy* by W. Chan Kim and Renée Mauborgne, they talk about the fact that most markets are red oceans, full of blood because of all the sharks feeding on the same small pool of fish. The submarket is a very red ocean, which is why it can be difficult to have success there.

If you think about how these markets have changed over time, you'll see that the submarkets and niches developed as a reaction to those red oceans. The first person who taught health, wealth, or relationships was working in a blue ocean with no other sharks or competitors coming after their customers.

But people quickly saw the success, so they jumped into the waters, too. Over time, the waters grew red with sharks feeding on the same customers. That's why it became necessary for people to create their own blue oceans. That's where the submarkets began.

The first teachers in these submarkets experienced great success as well, until people jumped in there and bloodied the waters. The smart people looked around and figured out what they could create INSIDE of their submarket that would become a new opportunity to those customers. They created a new blue ocean once again.

The mistake many people make today is they start looking at the niches, find one that looks good, and start building their company from there. The problem is that jumping into an existing niche is stepping into someone else's blue ocean. And if you are the third, fourth, or fifth person in that niche, then the waters are already starting to get bloody.

I suggest that you look at your submarket and try to create a new niche, a fresh blue ocean for yourself. Create a new opportunity for people so they'll want to dive in. This is what I mean when I say you need to carve out your own spot in the ecosystem. If you jump into an already existing red ocean, you'll be fighting an uphill battle. But if you create a blue ocean, you will find success so much easier.

CARVE OUT YOUR SPOT IN THE ECOSYSTEM

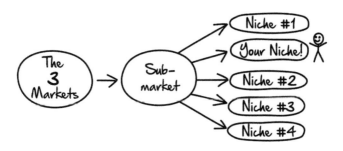

I'm sure that this makes sense to you conceptually. But in practice, it can be a little harder to nail down just the right niche—one that matches your superpower. When we get to Secret #3 later on, I'll show you how to identify exactly WHAT you are offering and HOW you are unique in your niche.

For now, here are some examples to help illustrate those blue oceans.

Core market → submarket → niche
Health → nutrition → high-fat diets
Health → weight loss → weight loss for college students
Wealth → real estate → flipping houses on eBay
Wealth → online business → Facebook traffic for e-commerce products
Relationships → parenting → dealing with teenagers
Relationships → dating → how to recover after a breakup

As you can see, you need to be a little creative to carve out your own niche, but it's the key to success, as you'll discover in Secret #3. What you have to offer must be different from everyone else in your market.

As you start looking around at the other experts in your submarket, you're going to find out who your competitors are, what they teach, and how they do so. Then you will start to see where YOU fit into this ecosystem. You want to create a message that will complement the other players in your market, NOT compete with them. If you do this correctly, all your big "competitors" will almost instantly become your best partners.

After I've identified the market I want to serve, I ask myself a few questions to make sure that particular market will be able to sustain my new expert business. Before I ask these questions, I usually back out of my main niche back to the submarket. I will be pulling people from the submarket into my new niche, so these questions relate to the people in the submarket.

Question #1: Would people in this submarket be excited about the new opportunity I'm presenting in my niche? Because you are pulling people from a submarket into your new niche, it's important to make sure they will be excited about what you want to share. You will be creating a new opportunity for them, and it has to be something that will make them interested enough to take action.

For example, let's say your hot market is wealth, your submarket is real estate, and the niche you are going to carve out for yourself is teaching people how to flip houses on eBay. Would people in real estate be excited about this new niche?

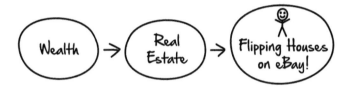

Question #2: Are the people in this market irrationally passionate? Before we ask how passionate the market is, I need to ask you a personal question. Are YOU irrationally passionate about your topic? When you hang out with friends or family members, do you always bring it up, even if no one else seems to care? If so, that's a good sign. But are there others as irrationally passionate as you? Here are some of the things I look for to determine if my market is irrationally passionate.

Communities: Are there online forums and message boards and social groups dedicated to this topic? How about Facebook groups and fan pages, YouTube channels, podcasts, or blogs with others geeking out on this topic you love so much?

Vocabulary: Does the market have its own special language? In the internet marketing world, you hear words like "autoresponder", "split testing", and "squeeze pages". In the health and biohacking market, they talk about "blood tests" and "ketones". An irrationally passionate market always has its own vocabulary. Does yours?

Events: Does this market have its own events? They might be online or offline conferences, seminars, summits, or masterminds. If events aren't happening in your market, you might have a hard time getting people to attend webinars and training. If they are already used to attending events, you'll have a much easier time.

Other Experts: Does this market have its own celebrities and gurus? There must be established experts already thriving and selling information products in your market. You don't want to be the first celebrity in a market. You want a topic or niche with its own subculture already established.

Go through these questions as many times as you need to in order to find the best market for you. I don't want you to waste any time, energy, or money going after the wrong niche if people in your submarkets aren't likely to follow you.

Question #3: Are these people WILLING and ABLE to spend money on information? Sometimes people are WILLING to spend money, but they aren't ABLE; they are broke. Other times people have all the money in the world; they are ABLE, but NOT WILLING to part with a dime. Your submarket must be both willing and able to spend money.

For example, I had a friend who saw huge potential in the video game market. He spent a fortune trying to launch his product in this new niche. What he found was that even though there were plenty of kids playing video games, they didn't have credit cards. It's hard to sell your mom on why you need to buy a course that will help you play video games better. Even though the kids he was targeting may have been willing to buy, they weren't able to.

But the opposite is true as well. One of my Inner Circle members, Joel Erway, started his expert business selling to engineers who had good jobs. What he found was that most of his dream clients did have money, but they were not willing to spend it on coaching. He spent almost a year trying different ways to sell his offers and had very few results. As soon as he started selling to a market that was willing and able to buy, he became an "overnight" success.

WHO DO YOU NEED TO BECOME AS A LEADER?

Jay Abraham once said that "People are silently begging to be led" and I believe that it's true. So how do you become the type of leader they need? I've come up with a few rules you can follow to become a charismatic leader for your movement.

Rule #1: Become an attractive character, and live the life your audience wishes they could live. In Secret #6 of my first book, *DotComSecrets,* I talked about a concept called the attractive character. We went deep into figuring out your backstory, character flaws, identity, story lines, and more.

We'll be digging into some of the elements like identity and story lines throughout this book, but I do recommend reading *DotComSecrets* to get a deeper understanding of the attractive character. The key is to understand that the people will follow you because you have completed the journey they are on right now, and they want the result you have already achieved. They want to become like you.

The gap between where they see themselves and where they see you is what moves them to action and helps them make the necessary changes. So if you aren't willing, or don't show them, both sides—where you came from and where you are now—then they won't take action.

That's why it's so important to live the life that your audience wishes they could—because that will inspire them more than anything you could ever say. Sometimes it's scary to become vulnerable and show your backstories as well as your life now, but it's the key to becoming a leader that will inspire people to change.

Rule #2: Maintain absolute certainty. It is said that in any situation, the person with the most certainty wins. I'm not talking about self-confidence. As my buddy Setema Gali says: "Self-confidence is for kids." If you want to make an impact, you have to be certain. Certainty is what draws people to leaders, to experts.

Gaining certainty can take time. It begins with you sharing your message often so you can find your voice and become certain in what you are teaching. The more you share your message with others, the more certain you will become. That's why I encourage people to publish their messages and their stories daily through podcasts, Facebook, blogging, Snapchat or any other platform you prefer.

Some of you are better writers, and blogging will become your platform. Others are better through audio or video, and will likely be using platforms like podcasts or Facebook Live. The platform is less important than the consistency of your sharing.

Years ago, as I was trying to understand what my mission was and where I fit into my ecosystems, I set out on a journey to discover my voice. I started doing a podcast almost every day. I was publishing videos on Facebook Live and Periscope every day—even when NO ONE was listening. It's important to understand that when you first start, you are not posting these for your audience—you're posting them for you.

Eventually people will start to follow, but initially it's so you can discover your voice.

Publishing daily is important because you will quickly see what topics and ideas people respond to and what they don't. Soon you'll become better and better at creating and posting the things that people care about most. As you do that, your audience will grow, you will become more confident, and your message will become clear. Over time, that consistency will give you absolute certainty, and you will become your message.

Rule #3: Don't be boring. Your audience must be fascinated with you and what you teach. If you're boring, they're not going to connect with you. I've watched a lot of experts come and go over the past 10 years, and I have spent a lot of time trying to figure out why some of them last and others don't. The one thing I've noticed across the board with almost all experts who've had success and stayed relevant is that they are highly prolific.

When I say prolific, some people think I'm talking about producing a lot of content. While that is true, there is another definition for prolific: someone who has abundant inventiveness. They invent new, unique ideas all the time. That's the type of prolific I'm talking about here. To make the biggest impact on the most people, and at the same time make the most money, it's vital that you fit your message into the sweet spot on what I call the Prolific Index.

PROLIFIC INDEX

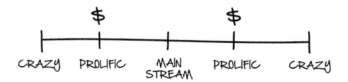

In the middle of the Prolific Index is the mainstream. This area contains all the ideas currently being taught to the masses in traditional mediums. For example, if you're a weight loss expert, the mainstream advice hovers around the government recommendations like the four food groups, or the food pyramid for nutrition. While some of these principles may be good, I'd argue that others are flat-out lies. Even if you believe those things are true, you aren't going to get anywhere teaching mainstream advice that people are currently getting elsewhere for free.

People can go to school and learn about all this stuff. It's common sense. It's not exciting. There's no money in the mainstream.

Now on both ends of this spectrum are what I call the "crazy zones". There are plenty of experts who live in the crazy zone. And while you can always recruit a few people into the crazy zone, it's difficult to get the masses to take action all the way to the left or the right.

One of my favorite examples of the crazy zone in the weight loss world was a documentary I watched called *Eat the Sun*. In this movie, they talked about how people can stop eating and just gaze at the sun. Yes, stop eating completely and just look at the sun. Kinda crazy? Well, the documentary did get me to spend a few minutes gazing at the sun, but I'm not crazy enough to give up food 100%. And I don't think anyone is going to make millions teaching that concept. (As a side note, I did actually love that movie.)

The sweet spot, the place where you will impact the most lives and make the most money, is right in the middle. Somewhere between the mainstream advice and the crazy zone is where you want to set yourself up. I call this place the Prolific Zone. When you're there, you're relaying ideas that are so unique, people will notice.

One of my favorite teachers in the weight loss niche is Dave Asprey from Bulletproof.com. His origin story falls perfectly in the Prolific Zone. One day he was climbing Mt. Kailash in Tibet and stopped at a guesthouse to shelter from -10-degree weather. He was given a creamy cup of yak butter tea that made him feel amazing. He tried to figure out why he felt so good. He soon discovered it was from the high fats in this tea, so he started adding butter and other fats to his coffee and teas. This experience eventually helped him create a national phenomenon called Bulletproof Coffee. People put butter and coconut oil in their coffee to lose weight and feel amazing.

For those of you who are just hearing this for the first time, it may seem a little crazy—but not so crazy that you completely dismiss it. And it's definitely not something the government is going to recommend. Bulletproof Coffee falls directly in the Prolific Zone, and its message has made Dave a multi-millionaire.

Did you notice how this message causes some polarity? The mainstream will probably hate it, yet there is something interesting there. When Dave tells the rest of his story and can back it up with science, it becomes a message that spreads quickly.

When your messages cause polarity, it attracts attention and people will pay for it. Neutrality is boring, and rarely is money made or change created when you stay neutral. Being polar is what will attract raving fans and people who will follow you and pay for your advice.

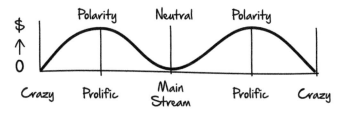

As you become more polar in your message, you will also notice that people on the other side of your message won't be happy about it. By creating true fans, you will always upset those on the other side. I wanted to warn you about this early, because often people (including me) really struggle when others get upset or disagree with their ideas.

For every 100 true fans who follow you, you'll likely get one person who doesn't like you. And for some reason, they always seem to be the loudest. If you search my name (or anyone's name who has tried to create change in others), you'll find tons of fans, as well as people who don't like us. It's just the nature of being a true leader. You've got to become okay with that, because without the polarity of your message, you can't get to your true fans and help create the change they need.

One tip I learned from Dan Kennedy that helped me cope with the small percentage of haters who will disagree with your message was this: "If you haven't offended someone by noon each day, then you're not marketing hard enough."

And Jay Abraham said, "If you truly believe that what you have is useful and valuable to your clients, then you have a moral obligation to try to serve them in every way possible." And that is why I am so aggressive in my marketing. I honestly feel like I have a moral obligation to share my message, because it's changed my life and I know it can do the same for others as well.

I want you to start thinking about your niche. What do you teach, and where is it on the Prolific Index? Many times, people are either playing it safe with the mainstream, or they are way out in crazy land where there is no money. You need to find your sweet spot between the middle and crazy land.

Rule #4: Understand how to use persuasion. Throughout this book, you will learn how to persuade people. In fact, everything you learn in both Sections Two and Three of this book are all about persuasion. But before we get too deep into that, I want you to understand the core foundation of persuasion.

One of my favorite books on this topic is *The One Sentence Persuasion Course* by Blair Warren. Blair is a persuasion expert who spent over a decade studying and using persuasion. During that journey, he broke down exactly how to persuade people in one simple sentence:

People will do anything for those who encourage their dreams, justify their failures, allay their fears, confirm their suspicions, and help them throw rocks at their enemies.

When I first read that, it made such a big impact, I wanted to remember it forever. So I made this graphic as a reminder.

Here is a quick recap of why each of these is so important. I included Blair's explanations as well because he explains these concepts so masterfully.

Encourage their dreams. As the leader, it's vital that you first understand your audience's dreams, then encourage them inside the new opportunity you are creating for them.

Parents often discourage their children's dreams "for their own good" and attempt to steer them toward more "reasonable" goals. And children often accept this as normal until others come along who believe in them and encourage their dreams.

When this happens, who do you think has more power? Parents or strangers?

Justify their failures. Most people who become followers and then fans will have tried to make a change before. You will not be the first person they have tried to learn from. For some reason, they didn't get their needs met from any prior encounters. It's important that you take the blame for past failures off their shoulders and place it back onto the old opportunities they attempted in the past. This way, they will be more open to trying your new opportunity.

> While millions cheer Dr. Phil as he tells people to accept responsibility for their mistakes, millions more are looking for someone to take the responsibility OFF their shoulders. To tell them that they are not responsible for their lot in life. And while accepting responsibility is essential for gaining control of one's own life, assuring others they are NOT RESPONSIBLE is essential for gaining influence over theirs. One need look no further than politics to see this powerful game played at its best.

Allay their fears. To allay is to diminish or put to rest. If you can put their fears to rest and give them hope, they will follow you to the ends of the Earth and back again.

> When we are afraid, it is almost impossible to concentrate on anything else. And while everyone knows this, what do we do when someone else is afraid and we need to get their attention? That's right. We *tell* them not to be afraid and expect that to do the trick. Does it work? Hardly. And yet we don't seem to notice. We go on as if we'd solved the problem and the person before us fades further away. But there are those who

do realize this and pay special attention to our fears. They do not tell us not to be afraid. They work with us until our fear subsides. They present evidence. They offer support. They tell us stories. But they do not *tell* us how to feel and expect us to feel that way. When you are afraid, which type of person do you prefer to be with?

Confirm their suspicions. Your audience is already suspicious of you and others in your market. They want to believe change is possible. But they're skeptical about making the leap forward. When you can confirm in story format that you had similar suspicions and describe how you overcame them, it will bond people to you.

One of our favorite things to say is "I knew it." There is just nothing quite like having our suspicions confirmed. When another person confirms something that we suspect, we not only feel a surge of superiority, we feel attracted to the one who helped make that surge come about. Hitler "confirmed" the suspicions of many Germans about the cause of their troubles and drew them further into his power by doing so. Cults often confirm the suspicions of prospective members by telling them that their families are out to sabotage them. It is a simple thing to confirm the suspicions of those who are desperate to believe them.

Throw rocks at their enemies. One big key to growing your following is creating "Us vs. Them" within your community. Take a stand for what you believe, why you're different, and who you're collectively fighting against. Why is your movement better than the alternatives?

Nothing bonds like having a common enemy. I realize how ugly this sounds and yet it is true just the same. Those who understand this can utilize this. Those who don't understand it, or worse, understand but refuse to address it, are throwing away one of the most effective ways of connecting with others. No matter what you may think of this, rest assured that people have enemies. All people. It has been said that everyone you meet is engaged in a great struggle. The thing they are struggling with is their enemy. Whether it is another individual, a group, an illness, a setback, a rival philosophy or religion, or what have you, when one is engaged in a struggle, one is looking for others to join him. Those who do become more than friends. They become partners.

Rule #5: Care...a LOT. The next part of being a charismatic leader is showing people that you actually care about them. There's an old saying that goes, "They don't care how much you know until they know how much you care." If your audience thinks you are just in this to make money, your vehicle for change will not last long. Your following will not grow. In fact, it will shrink very quickly. If you choose your ideal clients correctly, you'll have people you'd be willing to serve and teach and train for free because that's how much you care about them.

One struggle most of us have as we try to serve our audience is the guilt sometimes associated with getting them to pay you. There are two reasons it's essential to THEIR success that they pay you.

First, those who pay, pay attention. Over the last decade, I've invited my friends or family members to sit in on events that others have paid $25,000 to attend. Not once in those 10 years has a single one of those people who sat in for free launched a successful company. Yet in the SAME room sat people who invested in themselves. They heard the exact same information and, because they had invested money to be there, turned that same information into multi-million-dollar-a-year companies.

Yes, those who pay, pay attention—and the more they pay, the closer attention they pay. You are actually doing your audience a huge disservice if you undervalue what you are selling.

Second, the more success you have, the less time you will have. I remember when I first started, how proud I was that I answered all my customer support emails and talked (often for hours) to everyone who asked me a question. I thought I was serving my audience, but because of how accessible I was to everyone, I wasn't able to serve many people at all. You will need to put up barriers to protect your time, so you can serve more people. By charging for what you do, you are showing those who do invest how much you really care about their success.

Rule #6: Offer them value from their perceived relationship with you. They've subscribed to your list, they read your blog and listen to your podcast—they're hearing from you all the time. They want to see some sort of value in return for the time they are spending with you. And they want to get value as THEY define it.

One big mistake we experts often make is trying to apply what WE value most as OTHERS' standard for success. We are quick to define the value as some result we assume they are seeking, like "Make a million dollars" or "Lose 50 pounds". But that's not always how they define the value they want to get. Sometimes they just want to be part of a community. Sometimes they just want to get to know you. Some people love to consume and learn, and that's how they feel they get value. We can't push our definition of value on them. We have to allow them to feel that in the way THEY define.

I remember back when I joined my first mastermind group. We were at lunch, and my mentor, Bill Glazer, and I were discussing this topic. He said:

> You have to realize that people join mastermind groups for different reasons. Some people come because they want an

immediate return on their investment, while others are there just to learn. Others come because they want to show off. Some people want community. And some just don't have anything better to do. If you try to force "success" as you see it on them when they really just want to be part of your community or they just love learning, it's easy to alienate people from your tribe. They have to get value as they define it.

Those are a few of the keys to becoming a more interesting and charismatic leader. Understand, though, that you don't become that leader overnight. Start sharing your message and become consistent with it so you can find your voice. Figure out where your message can polarize people into true fans. Share your backstory and flaws. Be transparent. And over time, you will naturally become the leader your tribe needs.

THE CAUSE

The Cause
(Your Cult-ture)

The second piece you need in order to create a mass movement is a future-based cause. For every political, social, or religious movement throughout history, the charismatic leader paints a picture of the future they are trying to create and what life will be like when they get there.

As I mentioned before, my Inner Circle mastermind group spends a lot of time talking about building out your own CULT-ure. I hyphenated the word because I don't want you to look at this like a traditional business trying to build a customer culture. They're very different.

When I got serious about growing my company and taking my messages to the masses, I studied how cults (both positive and negative) were built. I discovered several common threads running through all their stories. Elements that are so much more powerful than anything you'll ever read about building customer culture in a traditional sense. We're going to look at these elements and how to include them in your business to create your own positive movement—your own cult-ure.

CREATING A MASS MOVEMENT

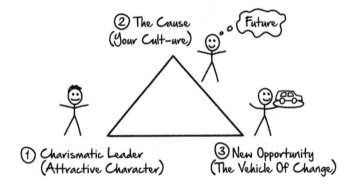

Our job as expert and leader is to help bring people to higher ground. To move them from where they are to where they want to be. In his book *The True Believer*, Eric Hoffer says, "Fear of the future causes us to lean against and cling to the present, while *faith in the future* renders us perceptive to change." In circumstances where people fear the future, they typically stop moving forward. For you to have success in this business, you have to give your followers hope of something better so they will be perceptive to the change you are going to offer them. You do that by painting a vision of the future that they want.

Most people want to cast all their faith and personal responsibility into something bigger than themselves. It happens in religion, it happens in political movements, it happens in the workplace, and it will be true for your movement as well. People want to plug in to something bigger than themselves, so it's your job to create that vision. Here are a few key principles that will help you create your future-based cause.

1. Where can they place their hope and faith? Earlier today, I watched the Star Wars movie *Rogue One* with my kids. Early in the movie, Cassian Andor is walking with Jyn Erso on the way to try to get a meeting with Saw Gerrera, who they thought would be the key to their rebellion. Cassian says to Jyn, "We'll give your name and hope that gets us a meeting with Saw."

"Hope?" Jyn asks.

"Yeah," Cassian replies. "Rebellions are built on hope."

Then later in the movie, when Jyn is speaking to the rebellion council trying to get them to fight before it's too late, she says, "We need to capture the Death Star plans if there is any hope of destroying it."

"You're asking us to invade an imperial installation based on nothing but hope?" they ask.

Then she responds, "Rebellions are built on hope."

Both those scenes were very moving to me, but as I thought more about that phrase, "rebellions are built on hope", I realized that not only rebellions but all mass movements are built on hope, and it's essential that we create that hope in the future, because without hope, they can't have the faith necessary to move forward and change. As they say in Proverbs 29:18: "Where there is no vision, the people perish."

If you have watched the elections over the past few decades, you'll notice that the candidates who win do so because of their ability to create a vision of the future that people want the most.

In 1992, George Bush had "A Proud Tradition" while Bill Clinton's was "It's Time to Change America." In 2008, John McCain was "Country First" while Barack Obama's motto was "Change We Need." In 2016, Hillary Clinton used "I'm With Her" and "Stronger Together" while Donald Trump said he would "Make America Great Again". Notice how the winners cast a compelling vision of the future, where the losers focused more on the present. (Interestingly enough, as you will see in Secret #3, both these winners presented a new opportunity where the losers were offering improvement.)

As we started to build our cult-ure within ClickFunnels, I wanted to create something that would unite all our members and give them faith and hope in their future with us. If I'm honest, I didn't know I needed this at first, and actually stumbled upon it one day. But the minute we discovered it, it instantly cast a compelling vision of the future and united our members.

We were about to launch our third annual "Funnel Hacking LIVE" event, and I was trying to think of a headline for the sales page. I remember reading a story about the late Gary Halbert when I first started my business where he said, "You are only one sales letter away from striking it rich." I know that for me, that statement created a vision that got me excited. I didn't know which sales letter or product it would be for me, but I had a perfect hope that if I would just keep trying, something would work. It created faith in my mind that what I was working toward was real, and even though I failed over and over and over again, that thought kept me moving forward through the ups and downs I experienced early in my career.

As I remembered what that statement did for me all those years ago, I started with that idea, and tried to figure out how to create something similar for my members. After thinking about it for a while, I eventually wrote out a headline that said, "You're just one funnel away from being rich."

As I looked at it, for some reason, I didn't feel it. I know that some people create sales funnels to get rich, but the majority of our members created companies and used sales funnels not just to get rich but, more importantly, to change the lives of their customers. So I went back to the drawing board. I wrote and rewrote that headline dozens of times.

"You're just one funnel away from quitting your job."

"You're just one funnel away from financial freedom."

"You're just one funnel away from growing your business to the next level."

"You're just one funnel away from sharing your message with more people."

The more I wrote, the more I realized that no matter what I wrote, it only would reach a percentage of my members. So I deleted the end of the sentence, hoping for some inspiration, and after sitting there for 10 or 15 minutes, I looked back up and saw something interesting. The headline read:

"You're Just One Funnel Away..."

That was it! Because having a funnel means something different to everyone, by not quantifying it, I left it open for their interpretation. So each person could finish the sentence for themselves. If their compelling future was to quit their job, then THAT is the future I'm offering them. If their compelling future is to share their message with more people and try to change the world, then THAT is the future I'm offering that person.

At our last Funnel Hacking LIVE event, I told stories that showed how this vision was true for me. I talked about each of the major failures that I had during my career, and how each time I was literally saved by a funnel. Twice I've been on the brink of bankruptcy, and both times, one funnel got me back to the top. Multiple times I've made poor decisions that could have (and probably should have) ruined me, but a funnel saved me. I shared story after story about how that was true for me, in a hope that it would give them hope of what's possible.

I now use that message in all my communication with my audience. I sign off in my videos by saying, "Remember, you're just one funnel away!" I've added it at the end of every email I send out. It's the theme of our events. It's a constant and consistent call out to our tribe, reminding them of the vision that they have put their faith and hope into.

To create this, I want you to imagine that you're running for president, and think about what the slogan would be for your campaign. What do your people really want? Where do they want to go? How can you capture that in a simple calling you could put on a campaign sign?

2. Help Them Break Their 4-Minute Mile I'm sure most of you are familiar with the story of Roger Bannister who broke the 4-minute mile on May 6, 1954. Prior to that, everyone thought it was impossible, and after Roger broke it, proving it was possible, many people since then have been able to do it. The certainty people get when they see someone else do something they thought was impossible, gives them the belief they need to also achieve that same goal.

On August 17, 2004, a similar record was shattered that gave me the belief that I needed to chase after my dreams. I had started my online business in 2002 while I was wrestling and going to school. My beautiful new bride was supporting her jobless student athlete, and I felt guilty because I wanted to help provide. But NCAA rules kept me from having a real job, so I turned to the internet with a goal to make an extra $1,000 per month. If my little business could do that, then I would feel like a success.

For about two years I was learning how this game was played, and had a few small successes, like my potato gun DVD, but nothing huge. At about that time, I heard about an online marketer named John Reese who was about to launch a new product he had created called "Traffic

Secrets." I heard rumors from friends that his goal was to make a million dollars selling that course. I didn't think too much about it at the time, but I was excited to buy a copy of his new course.

A few days before his launch, I went on a family trip to a lake in southern Idaho called Bear Lake. When I got to that town, I realized there was no internet access anywhere on the lake, except in a small library that had a very slow dial-up modem. About half way through our trip, I went into town and waited in line to get online so I could check my emails. When it was my turn, I opened my email and saw an email from John Reese with a subject line that said, "we did it!"

I wasn't sure what he was talking about, so I opened the email and read a story that changed my life. He said that earlier that day, August 17, 2004, they had launched his new course, and in just 18 hours, they had made a million dollars! As I read that, everything around me slowed down to a stop. He hadn't made a million dollars total selling his course, he had made a million dollars in less than a day! He had broken the 4-minute mile.

As I thought more about that, I realized that my goal to make a $1,000 a month was so small. I then realized that to accomplish this goal, he had to sell 1,000 copies of a $1,000 course. And suddenly, it became so tangible and so real for me, and I realized that that is what I wanted to do; I wanted to make a million dollars. It completely transformed what I thought was possible, and because of that, I started thinking differently and started acting differently.

Within a year of reading that email, I didn't make a million dollars, but I got close. And the second year I tried it, and I missed it again, but within 3 years, I had made a million dollars in a single year! Then later I made a million dollars in a month. And later we actually made a million dollars in a day! It was something that I didn't think was possible. It didn't make logical sense, they didn't talk about things like this when I was in school, but because John did it, I knew that I could do it.

I believe that every good movement has something like this that people can aspire to. Inside of ClickFunnels, and our Funnel Hacker movement, we created a club we call our "2 Comma Club." It is basically a free website where people can see pictures and stories about their peers inside ClickFunnels who have created a funnel that has made at least a million dollars. I want them to see that others before them have actually broken the 4-minute mile, and that they can as well. I want them to start thinking and acting differently, just like I did when I saw that John could do it.

You can see how we did this at www.2CommaClub.com, or by looking at this image:

What is the 4-minute mile for your movement? Initially, the 4-minute mile will need to be something that you've already accomplished, so you can show them it's possible and give them hope and belief that they can do it as well.

As you shift your focus to helping others accomplish the same results, and breaking their 4-minute mile, you'll notice something strange will happen inside of your movement. Your focus will be taken off of you making money, and into giving results to others, and for some odd reason, as soon as you make that shift in your thinking, almost instantly you'll start making more money.

I'm not sure why it works that way, but it always does. And as more of your members break the 4-minute mile, more people will be attracted into your movement and it will start to grow faster than you ever thought possible.

3. Let Them Self-Identify. Now that you've helped people to see the vision of where you are taking them, the next goal is to get them to identify with your movement. People need to be able to identify with who they are in your group, or there will be no connection with you or the other members.

When we first launched ClickFunnels, I created a webinar that I called Funnel Hacking, and during that presentation I first taught this concept. Later I started to watch as members of our group started to call themselves "Funnel Hackers".

I thought this was the coolest thing, so we created a t-shirt with Funnel Hacker on the front. We then started to give this shirt to everyone who opened a ClickFunnels account. People identified with that name, and it became part of who they are.

I even had one person who joined ClickFunnels, got the Funnel Hacker t-shirt, who messaged me months later. He told me that while he had never logged into ClickFunnels, he never canceled because he loved his Funnel Hacker t-shirt and felt like he was part of our community, and he didn't want to miss out on being part of our tribe. That was when I started to realize the power of helping people identify with your movement.

About a year later, at our Funnel Hacking LIVE event, we had ideas for 10 different t-shirts that we were going to give out to members who attended. We let our members vote on the saying that resonated with them the most. The shirt that ended up winning by a long shot simply stated: "I build funnels." It helped people identify who they are within our movement.

When someone joins you, they need to be able to identify by saying, "I'm a _____." When they can do that, they have an identity shift, which is very important. They get a new identity as part of the group. They become like a new person, putting the past behind them and looking toward their new future.

Brandon and Kaelin Poulin from my Inner Circle had built a good weight loss company based around her maiden name, Tuell. Their company at the time was called Tuell Time Trainer and they had built up a good following of people who loved what Kaelin taught.

I talked to them about this concept of getting people to self-identify with your movement, and they realized that, because of how they had named their company, it was very difficult for others to buy into it. Because her brand was HER maiden name, her customers could never identify with it. So while they followed her as a charismatic leader, she wasn't creating a movement. There was no cult-ure. I pointed that out at one of our meetings, and they knew that to get to the next level in their business, they would need to make a change.

As they were flying home from the meeting, Kaelin had an idea. She thought *Lady Boss Weight Loss. That's what it's going to be! Then they will say, "I am a Lady Boss."*

By the time they had landed, they had changed their messaging. They quickly launched the cult-ure, and within three months they saw their customer churn drop by 10% (which for them was equal to hundreds of thousands of dollars a year). On top of that, their TRUE fans—the ones who will purchase anything and everything they produce—now identify themselves as Lady Bosses and continue to grow by hundreds of new people every day.

Recently I've been working on a new supplement business, and I was trying to figure out what I could put on our packaging that would get our new customers to identify with our product and movement we are starting to create. The new product is an energy supplement called Ignite. I knew it would be hard to figure out who our supplement was for, because there are literally thousands of energy supplements.

So I started asking myself, "Who is this for? Everyone?" No, I needed to find my niche within the energy submarket. The problem with most energy drinks is that they're for everyone, which makes it really hard to compete. I know others target pre-workouts in the fitness submarket, but that's not who we were targeting either.

I knew that if we were going to have success, we needed to call out our people and get them to come to us. So I started to think, "Who are our people?" When we created the supplement, I thought it was going to be for entrepreneurs, so should we call it "Ignite: Energy for Entrepreneurs"? But then I realized that it wasn't just entrepreneurs. In fact, everyone who was pulling all-nighters when we were trying to launch ClickFunnels was using it, so it was also for coders.

And then, almost like a bolt of lightning, I had the inspiration. I remembered an old Apple commercial where Steve Jobs recited this quote:

Here's to the crazy ones. The misfits. The rebels. The troublemakers. The round pegs in the square holes. The ones who see things differently. They're not fond of rules. And they have no respect for the status quo. You can quote them, disagree with them, glorify or vilify them. About the only thing you can't do is ignore them. Because they change things. They push the human race forward. And while some may see them as the crazy ones, we see genius. Because the people who are crazy enough to think they can change the world, are the ones who do.

After finding that quote, I knew who our energy drink was for. Now we call it "Ignite: Energy For Those Who See Things Differently." People say, "Yes, that's me! I see things differently. I'm a rebel, an entrepreneur, a coder…someone who is trying to change the world." So that is how I create something that people can identify with.

To get people to identify with your movement, come up with something simple that you can put on a t-shirt your members could wear that would make them identify with your movement. Think "I'm a _____" or "I _____."

I'm a Funnel Hacker.
I'm a Lady Boss.
I build funnels.
I see things differently.
I'm a biohacker.

What would your tribe wear proudly on their chests?

4. Create your own Title of Liberty. In the ancient Americas, a military commander named Captain Moroni led an army into a war they couldn't win. Some of his troops started to lose faith in their mission, and some even left to join the enemy forces. The captain needed to do something quickly to save his army and his people. The story goes that he took his coat and tore it into a makeshift flag. And he wrote on it, "In memory of our God, our religion, and freedom, and our peace, our wives and our children." Then he put that flag on the end of a pole and called it the Title of Liberty.

When people saw it, they rallied around their leader Moroni, and in a scene that I can only imagine was similar to Mel Gibson's famous freedom speech from the movie *Braveheart*, they renewed their faith in the cause and went on to win the war.

TRUE BELIEVERS

Your cult-ure needs a Title of Liberty. Something they can look at when they're feeling doubtful—a rallying call. Something that will help them know who YOU are, remind them who THEY are, and refocus them on where you are going together.

There are different ways to create a Title of Liberty for your group.

Title of Liberty #1: The Mini Manifesto I got the idea for this one after I saw some of the cool things that Brandon and Kaelin Poulin were doing inside their cult-ure. They had all their women save this as the background image on their phone, so every time they turn it on (dozens of times a day), they are reminded what it means to be a Lady Boss.

12:00
Monday, January 1

*Lady*Boss

NEVER GIVES UP.
GIVES NO EXCUSES.
PUSHES THROUGH.
SPREADS SPARKLE.
GETS IT DONE.
TAKES ACTION.
IS CONFIDENT.
LOVES HERSELF.
KICKS BUTT.
STAYS FOCUSED.
IS UNSTOPPABLE.

It didn't take long after I saw that to create a mini manifesto for my Funnel Hackers and get them saving it as the background on their phones. Here's what we created:

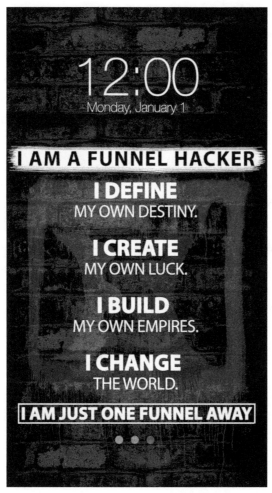

We took the phrase we created to help them identify with our group, then plugged in our core values to remind them what it means to be part of our tribe.

Title of Liberty #2: The Manifesto Do you remember the scene in *Jerry Maguire* where he stays up all night because he's inspired about how things should be, and he writes a mission statement that he calls "The Things We Think and Do Not Say"? He talks about what's wrong in their business and how things could, and should, be.

When I created our Funnel Hacker manifesto, I thought through a similar process. What was wrong in our industry. What were the things I hated about business that I felt weren't right for actual customers. A lot of it had to do with venture capitalists and how they destroy entrepreneurs and the cult-ure of those tribes. I wanted to create a divide between entrepreneural startups and VC-backed startups, something that my tribe would resonate with. It took our core values from our mini manifesto and made them bolder, something people would stand behind.

We then had our members print this out and frame it next to their computers, or make it their desktop background. That way, they'd never forget what we stand for. See our manifesto on page 45.

Title of Liberty #3: Video Title Sequence (More Advanced) All TV shows start with a title sequence that people hear over and over again. Think about the show *Friends* and almost instantly you'll be singing "I'll Be There For You" by the Rembrandts. What song do you think about when I mention the show *Seinfeld* or *The Simpsons*? These songs are burned into our minds and immediately take us back to the feelings we have associated with those shows.

I wanted to create something similar for the videos we created for our Funnel Hacker community, so we created a video that became our rallying call. When my cult-ure hears it, they are very clear on who we are, why they should be involved, and where we are going. People who resonate with it will join our cause; those who don't will be pushed away.

I've broken down the elements of my video into a script you can follow to create your own. You can see the video at www.FunnelHacker. tv. Here's how the script goes.

Identify the charismatic leader. Who are you?

My name is Russell Brunson.

Identify the movement.

I'm part of a group of underground entrepreneurs you've probably never heard of.

US vs. THEM

- **Take a stand.**

  We don't rely on cash from venture capitalists to get started, and we don't even have goals to go public either. In fact, our motivation is the exact opposite. We have products and services and things that we KNOW can change people's lives.

- **Why are you different?**

  Because we're fighting against the big brands, people with literally unlimited budgets, we have to do things differently. We have to do things smarter. We don't have financial safety nets. Every test we take is with our own money. We have to be profitable from day number one. So how do we do that? How is that even possible?

- **Who or what are you collectively fighting against?**
  If you asked the MBAs or look in the college textbooks, they'd tell you that what we're doing is impossible. Yet it's happening. Every single day. It's happening through the art and science that we call Funnel Hacking.
- **Who you ARE!**
  We are Funnel Hackers, and these are our stories!

Do you see how powerful that is? The video isn't long—only a minute and 10 seconds. But it clearly defines who we are and what our cause is all about. People who resonate with that message are going to say, "HECK, yeah!" and then join us. Those who don't get it will just move on. It's natural selection for the true believers.

Those are the four core things we use to create our future-based cause.

Where can they place their hope and faith?
Help them break their 4-minute mile.
Let them self-identify.
Create a Title of Liberty.

It will cast a vision, create hope, and give people the faith they need to move forward and make change. Now that you've got a charismatic leader and a future-based cause, it's time for the third piece of your vehicle for change—the new opportunity.

THE NEW OPPORTUNITY

New Opportunity (The Vehicle Of Change)

The last piece of the puzzle you need to create your movement is something I call the New Opportunity, or the vehicle for change that you are offering to people. This is by far the most important, yet least understood, part of the process. The difference between having some modest success and changing the world comes down to understanding and implementing the new opportunity.

When you study the successful mass movements of the past, you'll notice that each of the leaders offered their followers a new opportunity. Christ didn't give his followers a better way to follow Moses' law, he offered them a NEW law, a new covenant where salvation didn't come from animal sacrifices and following the letter of the law, but instead came from a broken heart and a contrite spirit. Hitler didn't offer the Germans a way to make Germany better or to pay off their war reparations faster. He told them Germany wasn't responsible for the first world war, and that he wanted to tear up the Treaty of Versailles and make Germany strong again.

In 2001, Steve Jobs stood in front of the world and told everyone he wanted to revolutionize the music industry. Then he pointed out all the "improvement" offers that promised to get us more of the same. You could buy a CD and get 10–15 songs. You could buy an MP3 player and get about 150 songs, or use a heavy hard drive that held about 1,000 songs. Each product improved the one before it, gave people more songs on one device.

Jobs wanted to create a new opportunity where someone could bring their entire music library—ALL their CDs and digital music—everywhere they went. And he wanted people to carry it inside their pockets. That's when he pulled the first iPod out of his pocket, showed everyone the new opportunity he created, and transformed the music industry forever.

He did it again when he made the announcement for the iPhone, and again when he changed how computers would work forever with the iPad. This pattern can be seen over and over again in business, religion, sports—anywhere there's real innovation in an industry.

In *The True Believer*, Eric Hoffer says, "The practical organization offers opportunities for self-advancement…a mass movement…appeals not to those intent on bolstering and advancing a cherished self, but to those who crave to be rid of an unwanted self."

Our goal is not to fix what's not working. Our goal is to REPLACE what's not working with something better.

Most often, when people start thinking about the product or the service they want to offer, they start by looking around at what is already out there, and then they try to "build a better mousetrap". When you do that, you are not offering them a new opportunity, you are offering them what we call an "improvement" offer.

WHAT THEY REALLY WANT

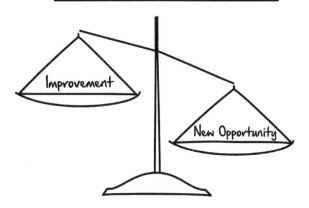

WHY PEOPLE DON'T WANT IMPROVEMENT OFFERS

Improvement offers are much harder to sell for a lot of reasons. Here are a few of the main reasons people tend to avoid improvement offers at all costs.

1. **Improvement is Hard** Most people have tried to improve in the past, and for some reason it didn't work. They've tried to lose weight. They've tried to make money. They've tried to make their relationships better. But if they're coming to you, then whatever they tried in the past didn't work for some reason. They know the difficulties they've had to go through in the past, and there is pain associated with that.

With a new opportunity, they don't know what the process will be, so they don't have to go through the known pain to get the result. Another amazing quote from *The True Believer*: "They must be wholly ignorant of the difficulties involved in their vast undertaking. Experience is a handicap."

2. **Desire vs. Ambition** All people have desire, but very few have ambition. My guess is that less than 2% of the population is actually ambitious. Improvement offers are selling to over-achieving ambitious people. If you do sell an improvement offer, you are automatically excluding 98% of the world. You will be fighting an uphill battle. A new opportunity, on the other hand, plays on people's desires for the change they want in their lives.

3. **Memories of Poor Past Decisions** If your followers are in need of improvement, they must first admit failure. In order for them to say yes to your offer, they have to admit that the choices they made in the past were wrong. No one wants to admit when they're wrong, yet an improvement offer forces them to admit they've failed. Remember the *One Sentence Persuasion Course* from earlier in the book? We want to JUSTIFY their past failures. A new opportunity does that.

4. **Commodity Pricing** When you are selling improvement, you are selling against dozens or hundreds of other improvement offers out there. You are stuck in the middle of a very red ocean, competing with everyone else selling similar options. This competition turns what you do into a commodity and pushes the pricing down. It quickly becomes a race to the bottom in terms of pricing.

Dan Kennedy once told me, "If you can't be the #1 lowest price leader in your market, there is no strategic advantage in being the #2 lowest price leader." In other words, if you can't be the cheapest, then you need to become the most expensive. And you can't do that when you are fighting inside of this red ocean. When you present a new opportunity, you are creating a blue ocean, and all price resistance goes out the window.

But the BIGGEST reason people don't want improvement offers is so important that I wanted to write a separate section about it. The #1 reason people don't want improvement, and the reason they will or won't join your cult-ure is STATUS.

STATUS: THE ONLY THING THAT CAUSES PEOPLE TO MOVE (OR NOT MOVE)

A few years ago, my friend Perry Belcher explained this concept to me. Once I understood it, I immediately changed how I interacted with everyone. He told me that status is the only thing that causes people to move toward you or not move at all. That's it. STATUS is the magic word in this business. When someone is presented with an opportunity, their subconscious mind is working on the answer to this question:

**Is this thing I'm considering going
to increase my status or decrease it?**

STATUS

Status as I'm defining it here has nothing to do with how other people perceive you, but rather with how you perceive yourself.

Almost every choice in your life has revolved around status—whether you know it or not. For example, what school did you go to? You (or your parents) picked a school because you thought it would elevate your status. Who did you date? Who did you break up with? Who did you marry? You pick those people based on who you thought would elevate your status. What school do your kids go to? What books do you read? What car do you drive? What car do you not drive?

All these things are tied into status. Almost EVERY decision you've ever made was based on this one subconscious question:

**Is this thing I'm considering going
to increase my status or decrease it?**

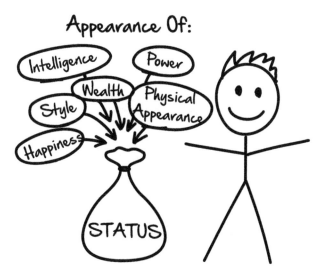

When we're looking at any opportunity, we have to decide if it will make us appear smarter, happier, more stylish, more wealthy, more powerful, or more attractive. All these things will increase status. If a potential customer can say, "Yes, this will increase my status." they will move toward it.

What stops people from taking that new opportunity? Fear of decreased status. The sale-killing thought is "What if I try this and it decreases my status? I will feel stupid." There's this balancing act going on in our brains all the time. We're balancing hope of increased status against fear of decreased status. If you're selling a weight loss solution, and someone has tried and failed on 27 different diets, that fear is going to be pretty high. You're going to have to work pretty hard to get the sale.

If your brain thinks that taking an action will reverse your status, then you won't do it—UNLESS it finds hope that by temporarily decreasing your status, you could increase it in the future. Your brain is always asking, "Will it be temporary and, if so, will the future gain in status eventually be higher?"

STATUS DECREASE

Feel Stupid

When people first find you and your offers, it's probably not the first time they've tried to solve their problems. They've tried to lose weight.

They've tried to make money. They've tried to do whatever your thing is. That's the big fear. I know if I invest $1,000 or $10,000 or $100,000 with this expert and it doesn't work, I'm going to look stupid. My wife or my kids or my friends are going to see that, and they're going to think I'm an idiot.

When someone invests in my $25,000 Inner Circle program, that money is leaving them, which causes an immediate decrease in status. But my members know that by taking that temporary decrease in status, the end result of being in the Inner Circle will be an increased status from what they learn and accomplish.

People are going to weigh the likelihood of success and elevated status against the risk of failure and the cost of that failure. Your job as the expert is to load up the elevated status side of the scale and decrease the risk of failure. You can do that by creating an amazing product and minimizing risk with things like money-back guarantees, risk reversals, and done-for-you options. The key to making a sale is 100% tied to this concept of status.

When people look at your new opportunity, that is the only real question they are trying to figure out. I like to think through what their perceived status is, and then try to make sure I add as many things

PERCEIVED STATUS

NEW OPPORTUNITY

STATUS INCREASE

① _____
② _____
③ _____
④ _____
⑤ _____

STATUS DECREASE

① _____
② _____
③ _____
④ _____
⑤ _____

possible that would make them increase their status, and then take away as many things from my offer that would decrease status. And so you can probably see why that is the BIGGEST reason why we don't sell improvement offers. For someone to say yes to that, they have to admit to poor past decisions and create a huge decrease in status. Then you are forced to fight an uphill battle that few people ever win.

So which factors elevate status? Well, it's different for everyone, but here are a few that are pretty universal.

- Appearance of intelligence (anything that makes them look smarter)
- Appearance of wealth, power, or happiness
- Physical appearance (weight loss, makeup, supplements, etc.)
- Style (think Mac vs. PC)

Now you might be thinking, "I'm not affected by status considerations. I like to drive a reasonable car and live in a modest home." If so, I'd like to pose a question. Why? Why do you like driving a car you feel is reasonably priced? Does it have anything to do with the fact that if you drove a Ferrari home one day, you're afraid that your friends, family, or neighbors would judge you? If they did judge you, how would that affect your status?

Status works on both ends of the spectrum. It's what makes some people fight for earthly possessions, and it's also what keeps others from desiring them at all. As much as we may hate to admit it, we are all slaves to what we believe other people will think about us.

WHY PEOPLE CRAVE NEW OPPORTUNITIES

So now you know why improvement offers don't work. Here are a few reasons why new opportunities DO work.

1. **New discovery** When people discover your new opportunity for the first time, they're going to want to share it because sharing something new gives them an immediate increase in status. Just think about when videos on YouTube or Facebook go viral. What's happening behind the scenes? I've worked with teams who create viral videos for a living, and they've found that videos go viral when they are cool and new because others want to be the first to show them to their friends. Discovery immediately increases perceived status.

2. **No pain of disconnect** Because they don't have to admit they made bad decisions in the past, there is no longer a huge pain of disconnect from what they are currently doing. They can just move on to something brand new. No pain of disconnect = no decrease in status. Improvement offers sell THROUGH the pain, where new opportunities sell AWAY from the pain.

3. **Dream replacement** One reason many people struggle to make the changes they want and need in their lives is the fear of failure. If they try to change and it doesn't work for them, then their dreams are dead. So they will give up potential success for fear of losing their dreams. We know that "without a vision, the people perish". When you make a new opportunity, you're giving them a new dream to move toward.

4. **Greener pastures** We've all heard a million times that "the grass is always greener on the other side of the fence", right? Instead of trying to convince people that their grass is green or offering to fix their grass, allow them to follow you to the other side of the fence. That's where they want to be anyway. Stop trying to make existing things that aren't working better, and focus on fresh, exciting, NEW ideas that will inspire people to follow you!

I hope by now you appreciate how important it is to create a mass movement for your cult-ure. When you have a charismatic leader, a future-based cause, and a new opportunity, you have the perfect environment for REAL change. Once you have that environment, you can get people to follow you and pay you so you can move them forward and change their lives for the better.

But most people get stuck here. HOW do you actually create the new opportunity? And if you are already selling something else, how do you reposition it to become that new opportunity for your movement?

CREATING THE NEW OPPORTUNITY, THEIR VEHICLE FOR CHANGE

While there are lots of ways to structure improvement offers, there are only two ways to position a new opportunity, either as an Opportunity Switch or an Opportunity Stack.

THE NEW OPPORTUNITY

① Opportunity Switching — Looking For Change
② Opportunity Stacking — Looking For More

Opportunity Switching Each of our prospects has a desire for some result, and they have been trying to get that result through some vehicle. Maybe they are trying to lose weight, and the vehicle they have currently chosen to lose weight is the Atkins diet. So my opportunity switch is to take them out of the vehicle they're currently using and put them into a new one. So in this example I could switch them from Atkins to something new, like the Paleo diet. If the Paleo diet has become a red ocean with lots of people teaching it, then it is no longer a new opportunity, and I need to create my own sub-niche like we discussed in Secret #1.

In the real estate market, they might be flipping houses or doing short sales. To create a new opportunity, I'm going to switch them out of those vehicles and into the new vehicle I created, which might be something like selling houses on eBay. Opportunity switching takes them out of the pain they're currently in and gives them hope for a new future through a new vehicle.

Sometimes the opportunity switch happens when they are moving from one niche to the new one that you created in Secret #1.

Other times it's actually switching them from one submarket to another. For example, maybe they are moving from making an income in real estate, to making their income through internet marketing.

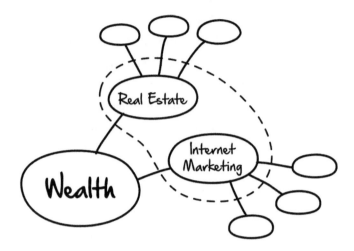

Usually the first thing I sell to someone when they enter into my culture is some type of opportunity switch. Sometimes the new opportunity is offered through a webinar, other times it's through a book or a video. It matters less what product they are buying; it's more important to understand that they are leaving behind whatever old beliefs they had about how to achieve their desired results and putting their hope and faith into this new opportunity.

Opportunity Stacking After someone has made the switch into your new opportunity, then all future sales to that prospect are typically an opportunity stack, not an improvement offer. I don't want to switch

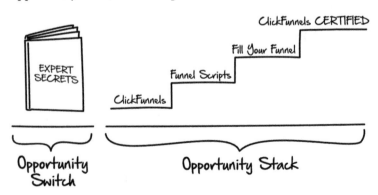

my prospects from opportunity to opportunity because it will cause confusion and break trust. But I can offer them an opportunity stack within the new opportunity that they have just joined.

If you've read *DotComSecrets*, you probably recognize the value ladder in the picture above. You'll notice that the first thing I offer people is this book, because it is an opportunity switch. I am trying to switch the career paths that you've been following up to this point (your current job, school, real estate, stock markets, or other ways to generate wealth). My goal is to help you see this new opportunity of becoming an expert and having a mass following who will pay you for your advice, and if I do my job right, you will make that switch into a career as an expert.

After you've decided to make that opportunity switch, then I will look for the other new opportunities within this opportunity that I can offer that will help to serve you at a higher level. You can see from the image that I will likely make you offers for things like ClickFunnels, Funnel Scripts, Fill Your Funnel, or my certification program. Each of these are new tools and opportunities within the expert business that will help you more easily get the results you desire within this new career.

I also want to point out that an offer can be positioned as BOTH an opportunity switch and a stack. It all depends on where a prospect enters your world. Some people never hear about this book, but they do find out about ClickFunnels or my certification program. When that's the case, that offer becomes the opportunity switch.

For example, when we launched ClickFunnels, we positioned it to speak to both types of prospects. For those who didn't know about funnels, I'd say, "If you've been struggling to sell your products online, you need to switch from your traditional website to a funnel" and then we'd offer them ClickFunnels. And for those who already had successful websites, I'd say, "You need to start using funnels so you can make money from paid advertising as well."

I did a similar thing when we launched our ClickFunnels certification program. We positioned it as an opportunity switch whenever we sold it to people who had any other type of job. We showed them how this was the highest paying part-time job in the world. And for those who were already using ClickFunnels or who were already consultants, we showed them how becoming certified would allow them to offer a new service to their clients. (When we get to Section Three on conversion, you'll see exactly how we speak to both audiences when we create our sales presentations.)

Now that you know why your offer needs to be a new opportunity, let's dive into how you can create that offer correctly from the ground up.

THE OPPORTUNITY SWITCH

So far, we've discussed the strategy for building a strong foundation so you can become a leader people will follow. You've chosen a niche you want to create. Notice that I didn't say "pick a niche". It's essential for you to create a NEW niche, a NEW opportunity for your people.

And you know a little about what you want to share. But so far you don't have anything to sell. The relationship between you and your audience isn't created until they pay you. If a tree falls in the forest and there's no one around to hear it—does it make a sound? I'd say no. Similarly, you aren't an expert until someone pays you for your expertise.

So where do you start? How do you create that new opportunity? Well the hardest way, where most people seem to start, is by writing a book. When you think about experts, that's usually what you think of first, right? They must be authors.

But there are a couple of problems with that approach. First off, it takes so much longer to write a book than you could ever imagine. (This one took me almost 18 months!) Second, I truly believe that you have to EARN a book. If I had written this book or *DotComSecrets* when I first had the idea over 10 years ago, it wouldn't have been any good. I needed to work with people for years in order to perfect my message. Only then was I ready to write a truly helpful book.

In the beginning stages of your expert career, you won't be good—and that's okay. As my good friend, Garrett J. White, once said:

> No matter what you do, in the beginning it's going to suck, because you suck. But you'll get better, and you'll suck less. And as you keep doing this, eventually you'll suck so little…you'll actually be good.

But you can't get good unless you start NOW. They say that the best time to plant a tree was 20 years ago, but the 2nd best time is right now. So let's get started.

The first step is to find a beta group to work with. This is your test group. You're going to serve them and get results for them, and you're going to work for free. I'll explain more about that in a minute, but first it's important to think through two things.

1. What is the RESULT you want for your people?
2. What is the VEHICLE or process you are going to take them through to get that result?

Once you know those two things on a basic level, you can move forward and design the perfect vehicle that your audience will love.

The Vehicle? ... The Result?

STEP #1: GET EARLY RESULTS BY WORKING FOR FREE

Let me tell you a story about a kid I met a few years ago named Alec Jetsel. He was trying to get a summer job the usual way. He filled out, 20 or 30 applications to different stores, but nobody would give him a job. It felt like he was just sending them into a huge black hole. He knew he would be the best employee any company ever had, if they would just give him a chance.

Then one day he decided to take matters into his own hands and actually prove what a good worker he was. He went down to the mall and walked into his favorite clothing store. This was his dream job—a company he would love to work for, but they had never given him a chance. He walked in and saw that some of the piles of clothes were unfolded and messy. So he went up to the manager and asked, "Hey, do you mind if I fold some clothes?"

The manager replied, "Why would you want to do that?"

My friend said, "Just because it looks like you need some help, so I thought I'd help you out."

The manager looked at him funny and said, "All right, if you really want to."

So Alec spent a couple of hours folding clothes and sweeping up, just generally helping out. When he was done, he said, "Thanks so much," and he left. Everyone at the store was kind of confused, but they were grateful for the helping hand.

The next day, Alec came back to the store and started folding clothes again. He spent another two or three hours helping these guys out. Then when he was done at the end of the day, he thanked everybody and started walking out. The manager stopped him and asked, "Do you want a job?"

My friend smiled and said, "Sure, I'd love one." And they hired him on the spot.

This is a perfect example of working for free to get a result. Alec could have tried to sell himself to the manager, but instead he proved his worth first. And he got hired in less time than it would have taken to fill out an application and wade through the interview process.

Another good example of this concept is my own Inner Circle coaching program. Before I launched it, I didn't have a track record as a coach for high-achieving entrepreneurs. Plus, I wanted to charge $25,000 a year for people to join. You could say I had a lot going against me. I could have done what most people do—put up a website and say, "Hey, my name's Russell Brunson. I'm the greatest coach in the world. You should hire me." But I didn't do that, for a few reasons.

First, no one likes to hear you talk about yourself. It's not cool. Second, I knew that it didn't feel right. I wanted to serve some people first and prove that what I teach actually works.

If you've read *DotComSecrets*, you know that one of the first things I teach people is to figure out who their dream client is. I already had an idea about the types of entrepreneurs I wanted to work with. So I started looking around for those people, and soon I met a guy named Drew Canole, the owner of FitLife.tv. He was a super cool guy and had a successful business in a market I cared about. Here was someone I thought I could help.

Eventually, a mutual friend introduced us. I went to Drew's house and talked with him for a bit. He mentioned some of the things he was struggling with. Then I asked him, "Would you mind if I came back and just worked a day for free to see if I could help?"

"Sure. But why would you do that for free?"

"If I am able to make a big impact on your business, then I'll probably charge a lot in the future. But for now, I just want to see if I can help you."

"What's the catch? What's in it for you?"

"There's no catch. I think what you do is awesome, and it'd be really fun to see if the stuff I do could help you at all."

Finally, he reluctantly said, "Sure, if you really want to, you can come out."

I think he still thought there was some kind of ulterior motive.

About a month later, I flew out and met with their whole team. We found that their funnels were making money, but they weren't profitable. I helped them fix their current funnels, and we built a new funnel for the upcoming launch of a supplement called Organifi.

Overall, between the day I spent in their office and the time going back and forth through email, I think I spent about a month coaching them through the whole funnel-building process for free. At the end of it, they launched their new Organifi funnel, and it absolutely blew up! They were making $20,000 to $30,000 a day, and it totally transformed their business. It was awesome! Last I heard, that funnel has done over $25 million dollars in sales in less than 3 years, and it's not slowing down.

I didn't ask Drew for this, but in exchange for my help, he made a video for me talking about the transformation his business went through and the results we got for them. After I saw that video, I knew I was ready to launch the Inner Circle, because I had proof. I had real results for someone besides myself.

We put the video into an online funnel and launched our new coaching program. People saw Drew talking about his transformation, and almost instantly the program started to grow. We set a cap of only 100 entrepreneurs in my Inner Circle at any given time and, despite the fact that we charge $25,000 per year to be a member, right now we have waiting lists of people fighting to get in.

The goal with this or any kind of business is not to lead with "How can I sell my product?" Instead, you want to ask, "How can I serve people?

How can I prove my stuff works? How can I get results for somebody else?" Those results are going to sell your products and services.

It doesn't matter if you're selling physical products, digital information, or service programs. Go out there and work for free. Get some results. If what you're doing works, then capture those stories and testimonials. Use them to attract and convert your dream clients. I'm going to show you exactly how to find that first beta group shortly.

STEP #2: DESIGN THE VEHICLE (YOUR NEW OPPORTUNITY)

The next questions are where do you find people to serve, and what should you create to teach them? Allow me to walk you through the process I've been using to answer those questions for over a decade. This process gets the results that you can then build an empire on. You're going to deliver a six-week opportunity switch masterclass.

During this masterclass, you are going to teach a small group of people about your new opportunity and how it will give them the end result they desire most. Start by picking a six-week window when you can deliver your class. After more than a decade of delivering online classes, I've found that six weeks is the optimum amount of time. Any less than that, and you run the risk of people wanting refunds (especially if the class ends inside a 30-day guarantee window). Any longer than that, and people will start complaining because they feel like it's never going to end.

I know we're not selling anything yet, but this beta masterclass will become the core curriculum for the people who will be paying you soon, so it's important to set it up in the same way that others will experience it in the future.

The next step is to begin building some of the marketing materials for the class. I know that seems backward. Most people design the class first and then think about marketing, but that is a formula for disaster. Just bear with me, and you'll soon understand why I do it this way.

Who / What Statement As a first step, I like to make a Who / What statement that quickly addresses which submarket my message is for, and what new opportunity they will be switching to. It reads like this: "I am going to teach _____ how to _____."

Here are two examples of what that statement could look like.

- "I am going to teach real estate investors how to make money flipping houses on eBay."
- "I am going to teach people who are trying to lose weight how to stop dieting and start drinking ketones for energy and weight loss."

The Opportunity Switch Headline Now that you know the WHO and WHAT, you need to give the class a sexy title that will attract your dream customers. I try to create a title that focuses on the result this workshop will deliver. I do that by filling in this phrase:

How to [*result they desire most*] Without [*thing they fear most*]

So for my ClickFunnels masterclass, I could create something like this:

**How to Create a 7-Figure Funnel in Less Than 30 Minutes
Without Having to Hire, or Be Held Hostage by, a Tech Guy**

Or if my niche were "flipping houses on eBay", the title of my masterclass would be something like:

How to Make a Quick $10k This Weekend by Flipping Your First House On eBay Without Getting a Loan From a Bank

If I created a niche for helping kids with ADHD, the title could be:

How to Naturally Destroy Your Kid's ADHD and Help Them Get Better Grades Without Giving Up Their Favorite After-School Snacks

If I were a relationship coach:

How to Reconnect With Your Wife and Find the Passion in Your Marriage Without Having to Go Through Painful Counseling or Wasting Time Talking

If I were selling weight loss through ketosis, I'd use something like:

How to Stop Exercising and Still Lose Weight Through a Little-Known Trick That Almost Instantly Puts Your Body into Ketosis, Without Giving Up Your Favorite Carbs

You can plug most opportunity switch masterclasses into that framework, and create quick titles that people will be interested in.

The 5 Curiosity Hooks / Getting Out of The Red Ocean Okay, you've written down WHO you're going to serve and WHAT the vehicle is. Next you need to make that new opportunity as sexy and exciting as possible. You have to figure out the big idea that will draw people to you. Why would they shift from the current vehicle they're in to yours? They will switch if you position your opportunity so people will believe—and buy.

A while back, one of my friends Jason Fladlien, author of the book *Webinar Pitch Secrets 2.0*, he taught me a concept called the five curiosity hooks. These are just different ways to present an opportunity. It's possible that all these hooks will work for your masterclass, but you need to pick just one for now that's going to work the best for positioning you and your new opportunity.

Here are the five hooks.

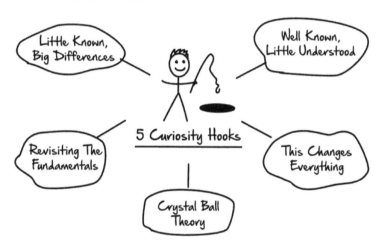

Let's look at an example where the new niche is weight loss through ketosis (Health → Weight Loss → Ketosis) to illustrate how you would position it for each of the curiosity hooks.

1. Little-Known, Big Differences This hook shows people something they aren't aware of and how knowing it could make all the difference between success and failure.

There's this little-known thing called ketosis. Hardly anybody is talking about it. But when you learn it and use it, you'll see a huge difference in your energy levels and how fast you can lose weight.

2. Well Known, Little Understood Here is where you take something that everyone THINKS they know about, and show how they're actually sabotaging their success because they're missing little nuances or details.

Everyone's talking about low-carb diets, right? We all know that refined sugar and carbs are bad for us. But what almost no one understands about low-carb diets is the concept of ketosis. It's not restricting carbs that helps you lose weight, it's getting your body into ketosis. And that can happen even if you are eating carbs—as long as you're drinking ketones.

3. This Changes Everything With this hook, something new has just happened in your submarket. It's related to the problem your audience wants to solve, and letting them know that if they aren't aware of it, they're at risk of missing out big-time.

Are you trying to stick to a low-carb diet, but finding the cravings are just too much? Do you start fresh every Monday, fail, then vow to start again with the same old strategy? You need to learn about a new type of ketones that instantly puts your body into ketosis, kills your cravings, and helps you lose weight easily. This changes everything!

4. The Crystal Ball Theory This angle shows how something that's been done successfully in the past is about to be made obsolete. You're persuading them that soon this will be common knowledge, but they can get in now and have early success.

Are you tired of dieting and counting calories, but not seeing the scale budge an ounce? Research is showing that low-carb diets just aren't enough, and staying in a state of ketosis is almost impossible for average people. The diet of the future takes low-carb to the next level—you can drink ketones and instantly put your body into ketosis.

5. Revisiting the Fundamentals This hook takes the approach that things are getting way too complicated, advanced, or sophisticated for the average person. Your new opportunity, on the other hand, takes things back to basics.

Do you spend hours logging every morsel you eat, every second of exercise, and ounce of water you drink? Diet trends have really gotten out of control lately. It's time to go back to the basics. With the ketosis diet, you only have to do two things. Drink your ketone drink in the morning and again at night, keep your carbs below 20g per day, and you're good to go.

Those are the five curiosity hooks. You'll probably notice that each one is speaking AGAINST a current red-ocean tactic that currently exists in the marketplace. By changing your positioning, you'll pull your opportunity out of a red ocean and plunk it down into a blue ocean. All you need to do is figure out which of the curiosity hooks makes the most sense for you, and that will become the hook for your masterclass.

Let's Review Take a few minutes and write down your own statements based on the descriptions above. When you're finished, you should have something like this:

- **Who / What Statement:** I am going to teach people who are trying to lose weight how to stop dieting and start drinking ketones for energy and weight loss.
- **The Opportunity Switch Headline:** How to Stop Exercising and Still Lose Weight Through a Little-Known Trick That Almost Instantly Puts Your Body into Ketosis, Without Giving Up Your Favorite Carbs
- **Curiosity Hook:** There's this little-known thing called ketosis. Hardly anybody is talking about it. But when you learn it and use it, you'll see a huge difference in your energy levels and how fast you can lose weight.

STEP #3: GIVE THEM WHAT THEY WANT (THE ASK CAMPAIGN)

At this point, it's important to remember that people don't buy what they need, they buy what they want. All too often we create a new opportunity giving people exactly what they need, a vehicle that is capable of getting them to their end result. But when they get into the vehicle, they don't see what they actually WANTED, like air conditioning, leather seats, radio options, etc. Because of that, they will leave before they ever give you a chance to take them to the result they really desire.

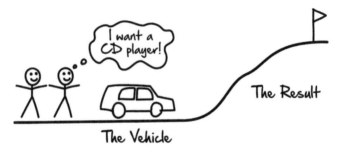

So in addition to providing them with their new opportunity, you also need to find out exactly what they want inside of that vehicle. If you do this correctly, they'll feel like they've found their new home.

You accomplish this by running a simple one-question survey we call an "Ask Campaign". The Ask Campaign is based on a simple three-step formula that I learned from two of my early mentors, Frank Kern and Ed Dale. This technique is SO simple, but don't skip it because of its simplicity. It's one of the most important steps.

1. **Find a hot market.**
2. **Ask them what they want.**
3. **Give it to them.**

That's it. Simple, right?

THE SIMPLEST BUT MOST POWERFUL FORMULA FOR SUCCESS

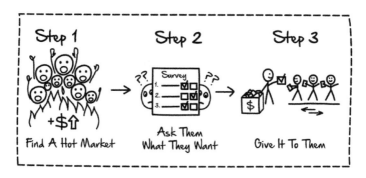

Because we're the experts in our respective niches, it's easy to assume we know what people want. And while sometimes we may be right, more often we miss the mark. (Probably because we are so close to our own ideas.)

For example, I own a company called OvercomePornography.com. When we started that company, we assumed that we were mostly selling to men who wanted to overcome their pornography addictions. But after running a simple Ask Campaign, we discovered that the people who responded were primarily wives and mothers who were looking for help for their spouses or kids. Just imagine how that changed the final product and how we sold it.

We used an Ask Campaign to collect lots of important information from our market. And we used that information to create a product people really wanted.

Let me show you how this works. First, you create a very simple page that asks, "What's your #1 question about _____?"

On the same page, I offer people a ticket to the beta group of my masterclass for free if they'll tell me their #1 question about my topic. The page reads:

THE ASK CAMPAIGN

Dear friend, I know your time is valuable, so I'll get right to the point. I need your advice. I'm putting finishing touches on a new course called "How to _____ Without _____". I want to make sure I don't leave anything out, so will you let me know your biggest question about how to _____? It could be anything. You may think it's silly. All you have to do is type your questions in the box below and click Submit. In exchange for your advice, I'll give you FREE access to my masterclass that's happening on (date). This course will sell for $197 in the near future, but you'll get special access to experience the course free when you let me know your #1 question. Okay, here is the easy form...

Getting your first 100 responses Once you have the web page set up (we have a template in ClickFunnels to make it super easy for you), it's time to start promoting it. Start by telling everyone you know. It sounds strange, but that's where I start every time I'm creating a brand-new niche. I post it on Facebook. I text my friends and family members. I try to get everyone I know to come to my very first masterclass. That's the low-hanging fruit.

Next, I start to look at the submarket that I've built my new opportunity in, and I look for people who are already in those submarkets. When I got started over 10 years ago, I used to look for forums full of people in my submarket. So if my new niche was about flipping houses on eBay, then I'd look for forums about real estate investing. I would become part of those communities and start participating in the groups.

Notice I didn't say, "Post spam messages about the masterclass." You need to give before you can take. So I go in and answer questions for a week or two. People see that I'm there to add to the community. And then, after I've become a familiar face who provides lots of value, it's usually okay to invite those people to answer my survey and take the masterclass for free.

WHERE ARE THEY CONGREGATING?

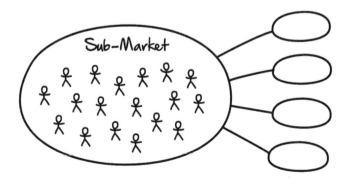

I don't use forums as much these days because most of that communication is happening in groups inside of Facebook. In the future, there may be a different platform where people gather in groups, but regardless the concept is the same. If you're looking for people on Facebook, search for groups in your submarket, and join the active groups. Then become an active participant in those communities and provide value. Then, when it's appropriate, ask people, "What's your #1 question about _____?" and post a link to your survey.

Of course, you can always run paid ads directing people to the survey, as well. If you're in a hurry, some Facebook or Google ads can get you answers in a hurry. But if you'd prefer not to spend money at this stage, social media groups work well.

Using the survey data Run traffic to the Ask Campaign page until you have about 100 responses. Out of those 100, you're going to find 8 to 10 core questions people are asking over and over. Those questions will become the titles of the modules in your masterclass. For example, when we ran the Ask Campaign for my "how to make a potato gun" product, people asked things like:

- What type of pipe do you use? Do the PSI ratings on the pipes matter?
- Which type of igniter should I use—barbecue or lantern?
- How long should I cut my pipes?
- What type of propellants should I use?
- Am I going to die if I make the gun wrong?

Next I found the most common 6–8 questions people were asking and created an outline.

- Module #1: How to Decide Which Type of Gun You Want to Create
  - What's a pneumatic gun?
  - What size gun should we build?
  - How do you build a bolt-action spud gun?
- Module #2: How to Pick the Right Pipes
  - What type of pipe do you use?
  - Do the PSI ratings on the pipes matter?
- Module #3: How to Find Accessories Before You Start Building
  - What type of igniter should I use?
  - Barbecue lighter or lantern igniter?
- Module #4: How to Cut the Right Barrel-to-Chamber Volume Ratio
  - How long should I cut my pipes?
  - What happens if my chamber is too big or too small?
- Module #5: How to Assemble the Pieces
  - How do I assemble the gun?
  - What tools do I need to make my spud gun?
- Module #6: How to Increase Potato Flight Distance
  - What type of propellants should I use?
  - What if my gun won't shoot?
- Module #7: How to Stay Safe While Shooting Your Potato Gun
  - Am I going to die if I make the gun wrong?
  - Has anyone ever died from a potato gun?

After you have the questions and the outline, there's one more step that gives you a really cool asset to use when you start selling your masterclass in the future. People have just told us EXACTLY what they want to know, right? So take all the questions and rewrite them as bullet points to use in sales letters, ads, emails, webinars, and lots of other places.

Question: What type of pipe do you use? Do the PSI ratings on the pipes matter?

Bullet: Discover the only pipe we will ever use AND the secret PSI rating that will guarantee your potatoes go farther and your gun lasts longer.

Question: Which type of igniter should I use—BBQ or lantern?

Bullet: Find out which igniter we'll NEVER use (and hear about a scary near-death experience that kept us from ever using it again), and why there is only one brand we trust.

Question: How long should I cut my pipes?

Bullet: You'll learn the correct barrel-to-chamber ratio that will keep you safe AND help your gun shoot 25% farther! (WARNING: Even being ¼ inch off could make every potato you shoot a flop.)

Question: What type of propellants should I use?

Bullet: Discover the secret propellant we accidently stumbled upon (when we ran out of hair spray) that immediately made our gun shoot over 50 yards farther every time!

Question: Am I going to die if I make the gun wrong?

Bullet: Learn the safety secrets we use to make sure every potato gun outing is safe as well as exciting!

Rewriting all the questions into bullet points will help make what you teach SO much more exciting to your students. And it will make writing your marketing materials easier later on.

At this point, you have an outline, which is really a table of contents. You could write a book from here, if you wanted to. All you have to do to deliver an amazing masterclass is find the answers to their questions and teach them in a way that will facilitate the best results. The participants will be happy because you're answering their questions. You're giving them exactly what they want.

STEP #4: DELIVER YOUR FREE MASTERCLASS

To make running your first masterclass simple, you really only need two tools—a Facebook group and Facebook Live (both free!)

Set up a private Facebook group so your beta members can interact with each other. A group allows you to post content, give class updates, provide accountability, and deliver any bonuses. Later on, you can make a membership site and get a little fancier, but for now you're just looking at getting some results for a group of people with your new opportunity.

Next, you need some technology to help you deliver the masterclass. Recently we started using Facebook Live inside our member group to deliver the live training. It works really well, especially if you're starting on a budget. There are other webinar platforms you can use as well. Platforms come and go, but my favorites right now are GoToWebinar. com or Zoom.us for webinars, or www.InstantTeleseminar.com for audio teleseminars.

You'll also need to let people know how to access the class. When is it being held? Where do they log in? What materials might they need to bring? You can give them the information inside your private Facebook group.

As for teaching the actual class, everyone has a different teaching style. You might decide to use PowerPoint slides and a webinar format, or you might just want to talk on the phone with a teleseminar format. And while I don't think it matters what format you actually teach it in, I do highly recommend using the storytelling skills that you'll be learning in Section Two of this book to get people to listen and make lasting changes.

So now that you have your vehicle for change in a newly created blue-ocean niche and a beta group of members you can start getting results for, you may be thinking, "But Russell, when do I start making money?" We're going to start addressing that in the next section.

After you've completed your masterclass, you will have some great results that prove what you can do for people. That's the goal from this first section. The results you get from this beta group will become the fuel that grows your expert business.

SECTION TWO

CREATING BELIEF

The first section of this book was all about understanding who you must become and what you must create to start building your mass movement. In this section, we shift focus to how you create certain beliefs in the minds of your followers. These beliefs allow them to be more receptive to the opportunities you're offering. When people have absolute belief in what you are telling them, you can positively influence them.

The longer I work in this business, the more I realize how everything comes down to one thing—belief.

Belief creates the customer.

Belief creates the results.

You must persuade people to believe in what you are doing, and you do that by mastering the art of storytelling. Secrets #5 through #10 will give you the foundation you need to tell stories that make your audience believe.

SECRET #5

THE BIG DOMINO

THE ONE THING

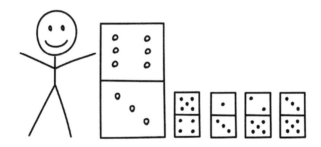

I was sitting in a room with about 120 other successful entrepreneurs, all of whom made at least a million dollars a year, a requirement to be in that room. One of the featured keynote speakers was Tim Ferriss, the author of *The 4-Hour Workweek*. After his presentation, he opened up the floor for questions. A woman stood up and asked, "Hey Tim, you seem to get so much done. What is it that you do all day?"

He paused for a moment, then gave an awkward half-smile and said, "If you watched my daily routine, you'd be bored out of your mind.

Most people wake up every morning with a task list of a thousand things to do. They go through the day trying to knock down all these things. I wake up every morning, and I meditate. I drink tea or coffee. I go for a walk, and maybe I read a book." He said he might spend three or four weeks doing that and nothing else. "My whole goal is to slow down and look around. Instead of looking for all the tasks that I could do, I try to identify the one Big Domino—the One Thing that, if I could knock THAT down, all the other dominos would either fall down or become irrelevant."

When he said that, I had an "aha" moment. I haven't yet figured out how to implement this in my personal life. But when it comes to how I sell things, he was 100% right. The first step to creating belief is figuring out the ONE THING you have to get someone to believe that will knock down all their other objections, make them irrelevant, or disappear altogether.

A little while later, I was talking to a friend and mentor, Perry Belcher. He told me how he had gone back and analyzed all the different offers that his companies had created and sold over the past 10 years.

He discovered that the more things they asked someone to believe in their sales pitch, the worse the offer converted. In fact, he figured out that if they tried to make more than ONE point or ask someone to focus on more than ONE thing in a sales message, conversion rates dropped by half! He then said, "Look at how many things a prospect has to believe in order to buy what you're selling. If it's more than one, you need to rework your sales presentation."

After hearing that, I knew we had to go back and look at everything we were selling. We asked ourselves, "What's the One Thing? What is the one Big Domino of belief that we need to knock down?" Every product has one Big Domino, One Thing that will knock down all the smaller objections and resistance—if we can get people to believe in that One Thing, then they will have to buy it.

I took a logic class in college that showed different ways to create valid arguments. One of the many valid argument forms is called "modus ponens". It looks like this:

If A, then B
A
Therefore B

If I were to put this argument into a sentence, I'd say something like:

If Dallin doesn't finish his homework, then he will not go to class.
Dallin did not finish his homework.
Therefore, Dallin will not go to class.

If you think about it, you'll start to see patterns of this argument everywhere. Religion is an easy example. In Christianity, everything hinges upon the truth of the Bible. If someone believes the Bible is true, then they have no other option than to believe that Jesus Christ is the Savior. If he is truly the Savior, then all the other concerns you have about Christianity disappear.

If the Bible is true, then Jesus is the Savior.
The Bible is true.
Therefore, Jesus is the Savior.

As a Christian, if I can get someone to believe the Bible—their one Big Domino—then it knocks down every other domino and makes any other argument irrelevant to the person who has that belief.

But it's not just in religion. We see this happening everywhere around us from politics to sports to the people we spend time with. That's why it's hard to have an argument with someone about something they truly believe in. When that seed of belief is there, it doesn't matter how much you try to convince them otherwise, it has already knocked down all the other smaller dominos that you're trying to stack back up.

The One Thing, aka The Big Domino Statement When we launched ClickFunnels, I tried to figure out the one key belief that I needed my audience to understand and believe. I came up with this basic statement:

> If I can make people believe that (my new opportunity) is / are key to (what they desire most) and is / are only attainable through (my specific vehicle), then all other objections and concerns become irrelevant and they have to give me money.

If I can get someone to TRULY believe that the new opportunity is the key to what they want the most, and they can ONLY get it through my vehicle, then they have no other options but to buy. This is the key to launching your movement. Belief.

Here is what I used for ClickFunnels:

> If I can make people believe that <u>funnels</u> are the key to <u>online business success</u> and are only attainable through <u>ClickFunnels</u>, then all other objections and concerns become irrelevant and they have to give me money.

When someone believes they have to have a funnel (and they do), and that I'm the only way they can get one, then they have to buy ClickFunnels. There is no other option.

I've helped my Inner Circle members create these statements for their businesses. We discovered that if we're struggling to make a valid argument that works, it's typically because we didn't create a new opportunity, but instead have an improvement offer. If we haven't created a blue ocean, then the argument won't be valid.

For example, I've seen statements that say something like:

> If I can make people believe that (cutting calories and exercising) is the key to (losing weight) and is only attainable through (my new weight loss course), then all other objections and concerns become irrelevant and they have to give me money.

That statement is NOT true.

If the belief you are trying to give them is that they need to cut calories and exercise, there are a few problems.

1. You are NOT in the Prolific Zone—you are in the mainstream.
2. This is NOT a new opportunity. There are thousands of identical programs crowding the niche of "cutting calories and exercising".
3. This is NOT a blue ocean. They could literally buy one of a hundred different products to satisfy the belief you created.

I would need to change my niche and my opportunity to be something like this:

> If I can make them believe that (getting their bodies into a state of ketosis) is key to (losing weight) and is only attainable through (drinking Pruvit's ketones, which put the body into ketosis within 10 minutes), then all other objections and concerns become irrelevant and they have to give me money.

The first step is creating your Big Domino statement. Once you have a statement that works and is true, the next step is to create real belief in your One Thing.

THE EPIPHANY BRIDGE

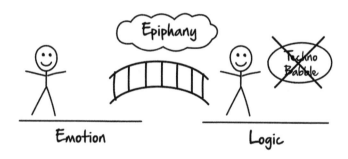

A few years ago, I helped a friend who was launching a new company. One of the guys working on the project wrote a script for a front-end sales video. The goal was to sell people into their new opportunity. After reading the script, I knew he'd made a huge mistake. He was trying to sell people on why they should join this new opportunity. Here's the email I sent him:

What I've found is that if you just sell something, it's not as strong, and doesn't create the emotion you need to really cause action. If you want people to adopt a new concept and want to get their buy-in, you have to lead them to the answer, but you can't GIVE it to them. They have to come up with the idea themselves. You plant the idea in their minds with a story, and if THEY come up with the answer, they will have sold themselves. The buying decision becomes theirs, not yours. When that happens, you don't have to sell them anything.

He wrote back, a little confused, and told me that my idea sounded like it came from the movie *Inception*, and asked me to take a shot at writing the sales script. I spent the next few hours writing an Epiphany Bridge script, which later helped that company acquire 1.5 million users in just three short months. That is the power of a story when you use it the right way.

So what is an Epiphany Bridge? It's simply a story that takes people through the emotional experience that got YOU excited about the new opportunity you're presenting to them. There's a reason you got excited about your new opportunity, right? Something happened to you at

some point in your life. You had an amazing experience that caused an epiphany. You thought, *Wow, this is so cool!* The first time I learned how to sell things online, I had an epiphany. The first time I learned about funnels, I had an epiphany. We're having these little "aha" moments all the time.

The first time you discovered your expert topic, SOMETHING happened that excited you. You had an emotional response that sold you on this new opportunity. Do you remember what the experience was? Do you remember how you felt?

That first "aha" moment created so much excitement for you that you started on a journey where you studied everything you could find about the topic. You started geeking out and going deep into the subject, learning all the terminology and understanding the science and technical aspects behind why it worked, and then you became logically sold on the new opportunity.

Now at this point you've had an emotional connection with the new opportunity as well as a logical connection. Then, because you believe so much in what you're learning, you have a desire to share it with other people. But unfortunately for you, the first thing you try to do is logically convince everyone you know about this new idea. You probably expected them to be as excited as you were, but quickly found out that they were resistant to the new ideas. Has this ever happened to you?

The problem is that you started to speak a language we call "technobabble". One of my friends, Kim Klaver, wrote a book called *If My Product's So Great, How Come I Can't Sell It?* In it, she identifies technobabble as the #1 sales killer.

We all love our ideas so much. We want people to understand why they should follow us and use our products and services. But for some reason, as soon as we try to explain our beliefs to someone, we automatically start to spew the technobabble we've learned, in order to logically convince people to buy. We talk about why this concept is the best and potentially mention all the science behind what we do. We talk about how we're "leading the industry" with "ground-breaking" products. We share industry numbers and jargon.

But all the logical stuff that strengthened our own beliefs in the new opportunity will not help people buy unless they've ALREADY HAD THE SAME INITIAL EMOTIONAL EPIPHANY that you had. All the logic, features, and benefits you give people before the epiphany will just annoy them. It's frustrating and often completely offensive. There's a time and a place for logic, but you have to convince them emotionally first, before they'll be excited by your logic.

THE EPIPHANY BRIDGE

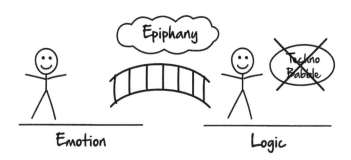

Think about it. YOU didn't buy into the new opportunity because of all the logical technobabble. You bought in because of some emotional experience that happened BEFORE you geeked out. You had an epiphany FIRST, and that caused you to move forward. People don't buy logically, they buy based on emotion. Then they use logic to justify the purchase decision they've already made.

For example, let's say I purchased a Ferrari. I am emotionally invested in the feeling I want to have when I'm driving it. That's why I bought the Ferrari (or a big house, expensive clothes, watches, etc.) But then I have to logically justify to myself, my friends, or my spouse why it was worth spending all that money. I have to explain how it gets better gas mileage, it was on sale, it came with a great warranty. Logic is justification for the emotional attachment I've already made.

If you think about it, there's a status consideration on BOTH sides of this equation. I'm emotionally attached to the status that the new Ferrari will give me, but then I need to justify it logically to my friends and family so I don't lose status in their minds. But good luck selling me logically if I don't already have the emotional connection with that car—it's pretty much impossible.

Logic doesn't sell.

Emotions sell.

So to create those emotions, you have to go back and remember what it was that gave YOU the epiphany that caused you to believe in the new opportunity. That story—your Epiphany Bridge story—provides the emotional connection, and bridges the gap from the emotional to the logical side.

If you can tell a story about how you got your big "aha", and if you structure the story right, they will have the same epiphany and will sell themselves on your product or service. Then they'll look for ways to logically justify the purchase and learn all the technobabble on their own. Your job is to learn how to tell these stories in a way that will lead people to the epiphany, and they will do the rest.

So my first question for you is "What was your core Epiphany Bridge story that convinced you of the One Thing you are sharing with others?" We'll worry about how to structure that story over the next two secrets, but for now, I want you to think back to the original experience that gave you your first epiphany, that brought you on this journey.

Do you remember what happened? What was happening around you? How did you feel? It's important to remember those details, because they are the key to telling a good story.

EFFECTIVE STORYTELLING

Have you ever noticed that two people can tell the same story with completely different outcomes? In one, you're emotionally captivated and engaged. Then someone else tells you a story about the exact same experience and you fall asleep. What's the difference? What makes some people better storytellers than others?

There are lots of reasons, but you don't have to know them all to tell a great story that gets prospects to buy. It only takes a couple of things to really make a captivating and interesting story.

The first key to telling captivating stories is oversimplification. When you're telling stories, you need to speak at about a third-grade level. Many of you will struggle with this because you like to use big words and show off your vocabulary and try to sound sophisticated and smart. There may be a time and a place for that, but it's not when you're telling stories. People are used to digesting information at about a third-grade level. When you go above that, you start losing people quickly. There is a reason the news stations speak to their audiences at this level.

During the 2016 primary elections, a study looked at the speeches of the Republican candidates and ran them through the Flesch-Kincaid test that shows the grade level of their speech. Trump averaged a third- to fourth-grade level on each of his speeches, where other candidates like Ted Cruz had a ninth-grade level and both Ben Carson and Mike Huckabee were at an eighth-grade level. Using big words may make you feel smarter, but it will not influence others.

But sometimes you have to talk about complex ideas. So how do you take a complicated idea and simplify it quickly? You do this using a

"KINDA LIKE" BRIDGE

What They Understand   It's kinda like...   New Concept

tool I created called a "kinda like" bridge. Every time I run into a word or a concept that is past a third-grade level, I stop and think about how I can relate that concept to something they already know and understand. The same way I would try to explain complex ideas to my kids.

For example, in one of my sales scripts, I was trying to teach a process called ketosis, which is a way to lose weight. (That sentence right there was a mini "kinda like" bridge! Did you notice that?) In the sales script, I mentioned the word "ketones" and I watched as the audience zoned out. I discovered that if they don't know what a word means, they stop paying attention to everything you say afterward. So I started using a "kinda like" bridge like this:

> The goal is to get ketones into your body. Now what are ketones? Well, they are kinda like millions of little motivational speakers running through your body that give you energy and make you feel awesome.

I take this new concept or word that people may not understand and add the phrase "it's kinda like…" to the sentence. I'm connecting the new word or concept to something they already understand. Something that makes total sense to them, so they get it. My audience knows what a motivational speaker is. And they can imagine what it might feel like to have millions of little ones running around in their bodies.

In that same script, I was trying to explain what it feels like to be in ketosis, and that's a hard thing to understand. It feels good. It feels awesome! So I had to take this concept and say:

> When you're in ketosis, it's kinda like the old video game Pac-Man. Remember? You spent the whole game running away from the ghosts. But every once in a while, you get a power

pellet and suddenly you get tons of energy, and then you're actually chasing the ghosts, and you feel ON. That's what it feels like to be in ketosis.

Again, I'm taking this concept that's vague and hard to understand and bridging it with something they do understand, using the phrase "kinda like".

Any time you're speaking (or writing) and you hit a friction point where some people may not understand what you're trying to convey, just say "it's kinda like…" and relate it to something easy to understand. This keeps your stories simple, entertaining, and effective. Oversimplification is the key.

HOW DOES IT FEEL?

The next way to improve your storytelling is to add in feelings and emotions. In film, it's often a lot easier to get people to feel something. One of my favorite examples of this is from the movie *X-Men: First Class*. In this movie, we are taken back into the X-Men's past and given a glimpse of what it was like for them growing up and discovering their powers.

There was a scene where young Magneto was taken to a Nazi concentration camp, and as they pulled him and his family into the gates, they noticed the metal fences around their compound started to move as he started to resist them. They wanted to see what his powers were, so they brought him into a very small room with a Nazi leader who wanted a demonstration of his powers. They also brought Magneto's mother into the room, so they could use her as leverage to get him to do what they wanted.

The leader points a gun at Magneto's mother and has him try to move a metal coin on the desk. He nervously tries to move the coin, but isn't able, so the leader pulls the trigger and kills his mother. And then you see a scene so powerful that, without a single word being said, you actually feel the pain that Magneto is going through.

You watch as his eyes shift from sadness to anger. He then uses his powers to crush a bell on the Nazi leader's desk. From there, he starts yelling and moving everything metal inside the room. He crushes the guards' helmets, instantly killing them, and then completely destroys everything in the room. And that's when he found his power.

When you're watching the film, you are able to see all of this happen without any words, because we can see his face, we can experience the room, we hear the music, and we actually feel, in some way, Magneto's pain and suffering. That is the power of films.

Now most of us aren't producing films to sell our stuff, but we have to learn how to tell stories in a way that help others feel the same.

Imagine if Magneto just came in and said something like, "Yeah, so when I was a kid, I was in a Nazi concentration camp and they wanted me to move a metal coin, but I wasn't able to do it, so they killed my mom. I was really mad, so I blew the whole place up."

Did you feel anything there? No, you wouldn't have had the same emotional experience that you need to connect with that character. Yet that's how most people tell their stories. If you look at a good fiction author, they'll have the character come into a room, then spend several pages describing the room. They talk about the lights, how things looked and felt, and everything they need to set up the scene. Then they go deep into how the character is feeling. And that is the key. You have to explain how you feel, and when you do that, people will start to feel what you were feeling.

For example, what if I tell a story like this:

I was sitting at home, and I could hear my wife and kids in the other room playing. They had no idea what had just happened.

I was sitting there freaked out because I knew the bills were due, but had no idea how I was going to pay them. I started to get a shooting pain in my stomach. It felt like a heart attack, but it was lower in my gut. I felt this pressure coming down and I literally felt like someone was sitting on my neck. It got so heavy that I couldn't lift my head. The only thing I could see were the palms of my hands, and they were sweating, yet I was freezing cold. My whole body was shaking and shivering because I was in so much pain and frustration, yet I was frozen with fear.

As you read that story, you probably started to actually feel the things I explained. How many of you felt a pain in your gut, or a weight on your neck, or sweaty palms? By explaining how I felt, you almost instantly will feel something similar. When I tell a story this way, I am controlling the state of the person listening.

It's essential that I control their state, and I do this by telling the story in a way that gets you to feel what I felt, so when I explain how I had my epiphany, you can experience the same epiphany. If I want you to have the same epiphany I had, you need to be in the same state that I was in when I had that epiphany.

Have you ever had the experience where you told someone a story about a situation that was really funny or exciting, and after you told it to them, they didn't quite get it? They understood, but they didn't "get" what you were trying to share with them. So you try to tell the story again another way, and then again another way, and after a few attempts, you throw up your hands in defeat and say something like, "Well, I guess you had to be there." That's what happens when you don't get people into the same state that you were in when you had that epiphany.

Now that you understand the basics of an Epiphany Bridge, how to simplify your stories, and how to get people to feel things when you tell your stories, I want to transition into story structure. When you learn the right structure for telling your stories and you apply the concepts you learned here, you will become a master at storytelling and story selling.

THE HERO'S TWO JOURNEYS

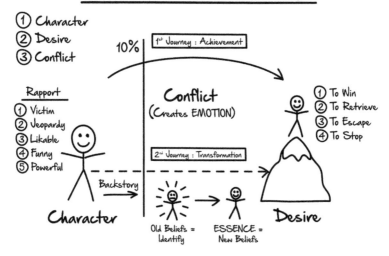

F or the past 10 years, I've focused on "story selling" to get people excited about the new opportunities I offer them. I didn't really have much structure. I just told a lot of stories and noticed that some of them encouraged my audience to believe and follow me, while others didn't have much impact at all.

Over time, I became better and better at telling stories. But it wasn't until I met a guy named Michael Hauge that I really started to understand story structure. Once I understood structure, I was able to craft stories so they always created the right environments for people to have the necessary epiphanies.

One of my friends, Daegan Smith, started me on the path to creating or changing beliefs with stories. He told me to listen to an audio book by Michael Hauge and Christopher Vogler called *The Hero's 2 Journeys*. Michael has been one of Hollywood's top script consultants and story experts for more than 30 years. He's the guy that top screenwriters and directors call to make sure that their movies are following correct story structure for maximum emotional impact.

Shortly after I listened to the book, Daegan and I hired Michael to speak at one of our events, showing us how to use stories to create belief in the minds of our customers. What he taught was fascinating, and helped me become a better storyteller. This journey has been a huge focus for me over the past five years.

I want to walk you through what I learned from *The Hero's 2 Journeys*. It will give you context for what a good story needs to be, and will help you craft your Epiphany Bridge stories.

Good stories are really simple. There can be layers of complexity, but at the core they are all very simple. Depending on the complexities I share, I can tell the same story in 60 seconds or 60 minutes—all with the same desired effect.

Every good story is built on three foundational elements (Character, Desire and Conflict), also known as "the plot."

THE HERO'S 2 JOURNEYS

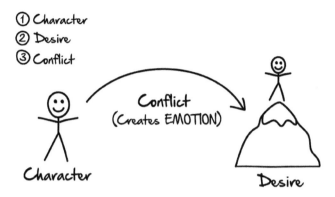

① Character
② Desire
③ Conflict

Conflict
(Creates EMOTION)

Character

Desire

Once upon a time, there was a girl named Red Riding Hood. She wanted to take a basket of cookies to her grandma, who lived in the woods. What she didn't know was that the big, bad wolf was waiting to gobble her up.

Character: Red Riding Hood

Desire: Take a basket of cookies to her grandma

Conflict: big, bad wolf

These are the basic elements of every movie, book, play, TV show, opera—any type of story. After showing me this, Michael explained, "Every good story is about a captivating character who is pursuing some compelling desire and who faces seemingly insurmountable obstacles to achieving it. That's it. If you've got those three things, then you've got a good story."

Your Plot Statement The first Epiphany Bridge story you will tell is the one that got you excited about your new opportunity in the first place. Take a few minutes to think about your story.

You are the character, so that step is easy. But what desire started you on your journey? What did you want to achieve? Write it down.

Next, what was the conflict you experienced along the way? Write it down. Boom! You've got a plot. Now write out your basic plot in one sentence, like I did for Little Red Riding Hood above. Here is an example:

> Once upon a time, there was a guy named Russell Brunson, who wanted to figure out a way to support his new family without having to get a traditional job. So he started selling information products (potato gun DVDs) online. But one day, Google's ad costs tripled, and his little business dried up overnight.

Character: Russell Brunson

Desire: Support his new family

Conflict: Google's ad costs tripled and his business dried up overnight

That is the basic structure of every story. When I'm first building out my inventory of stories (which you will do in Secret #9), I always start with a plot statement. This allows me to tell the entire story in just a few seconds, if I need to. Or I can fill in the details and talk for hours.

Now that you have the basic plot written out, let's dig deeper into each element so you have the tools you need to flesh out your stories and really hook into people's emotions.

1. **Build rapport with the hero.** The first 10% of any movie is all about building rapport with the hero, so we have a vested interest in their journey. If we don't build rapport with the hero in the story, then no one cares what else happens to them on their journey. If you do a good job of building that rapport up front, the audience will be engaged throughout the whole thing. You want people to get into a rapport with the hero

quickly. The fastest way to do that is to connect with two or more of these core identities:

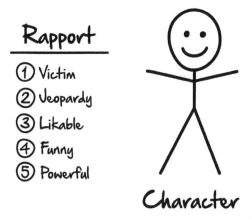

Rapport

1. Victim
2. Jeopardy
3. Likable
4. Funny
5. Powerful

Character

- Make the character a **victim** of some outside force, so we want to root for them.
- Put the character in **jeopardy**, so we worry about them.
- Make the character **likable**, so we want to be with them.
- Make the character **funny**, so we connect with them.
- Make the character **powerful**, so we want to be like them.

After you've introduced the identities, it's time to introduce the character flaws that have caused you (as the hero) to struggle. Sharing flaws is critical to gaining rapport. No one cares about Superman until we introduce kryptonite. He's an uninteresting character until he has flaws and weaknesses, and the same is true of any hero. Sometimes it's scary to share these flaws in your stories, but they are the key to building rapport.

2. **Introduce the desire for something more.** Every story is about a journey either toward pleasure or away from pain. The hero must have suffered some type of wound, or carry an unhealed

source of continuous pain, in the backstory. Because the wound has never healed, it causes the fear and pain that drive the character. Usually, the hero desires to accomplish something they believe will heal that wound. There are four core desires that drive most heroes. Two of them move the hero toward pleasure, and two move away from pain.

Toward Pleasure

- **To Win** The hero may be trying to win the heart of someone they love, or they may want to win fame, money, a competition, or prestige. But as you now know, they are really looking for an increase in status.
- **To Retrieve** The hero wants to obtain something and bring it back.

Away From Pain

- **To Escape** The hero desires to get away from something that's upsetting or causing pain.
- **To Stop** The hero wants to stop some bad thing from happening.

The story describes the journey to achieving the desire. But in all good stories, the hero is actually on two journeys—the one that everyone sees (The Journey of Achievement), and one that's hidden (The Journey of Transformation). The second journey may not be as obvious, yet it's the key to the whole story.

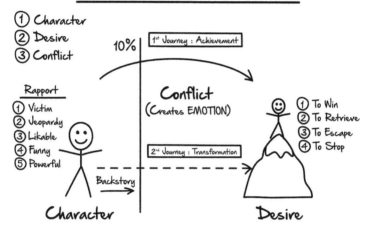

The Journey of Achievement This is the first journey, the one that everyone listening to the story is aware of. There's a visible goal with a finish line that everyone can see. It's the reason the hero sets out on the journey in the first place. The audience is rooting for the hero to accomplish this journey. While this journey is what drives the story forward, it's the second journey that actually matters the most. In fact, in many stories, the hero never actually achieves his end desire. Or if he does, he gives it up for the real transformational journey that he's been on throughout the story.

The Journey of Transformation During the first 10% of the story, we learn about the character and the beliefs they have that make up their identity. A particular identity is very important to the hero at the beginning of the story, but along the way they become someone else, someone better. It's almost like the death of their old belief systems, and the resurrection or rebirth of a new person. This transformation is the real journey that our hero has actually been on.

Old Beliefs = Identify   **ESSENCE = New Beliefs**

One of my favorite stories that shows this transformation of a character is from the animated movie *Cars*. Lightning McQueen has a very real goal he wants to achieve—to win the Piston Cup. The whole movie is centered around him getting to California so he can win. He stumbles upon conflict along the way, but eventually he gets to the big race.

In the last scene, he's racing and about to finally achieve all his desires, but then the car he is racing against (The King) gets into a huge wreck. McQueen's win is guaranteed. But because he's been on a journey of transformation, he chooses to slam on his brakes just inches before the finish line and watches as Chick Hicks races past him for the win. He then backs up, drives over to The King, and pushes him across the finish line.

The King then says, "You just gave up the Piston Cup."

To which McQueen responds, "A grumpy old racing car once told me something—it's just an empty cup."

Through this journey, he has been doing everything possible to achieve his greatest desires, and then at the last minute, he gives them up to become something more. We see the death and rebirth of his identity. We see the new beliefs he has created. We see his essence. That is the key to a great story.

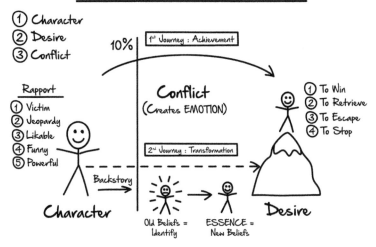

THE HERO'S 2 JOURNEYS

3. **Introduce the conflict**. Desire is essential to the story because it shows the end goal. It provides a reason for the journey to move forward. But emotion doesn't come from the desire. It comes from the conflict the hero faces while trying to gain the desire.

In pursuing the goal, there must be seemingly insurmountable obstacles. If it doesn't seem impossible for the hero to get what they want, people won't care as much. Our primary goal as storytellers is to elicit emotion, and you can't do that without conflict.

Michael Hauge showed me the patterns of conflict that are consistent with almost all Hollywood movies. There are five turning points that create the emotion in almost all films. As you review each one, think about every movie you've seen and how they fit into these five turning points of conflict.

5 TURNING POINTS OF CONFLICT

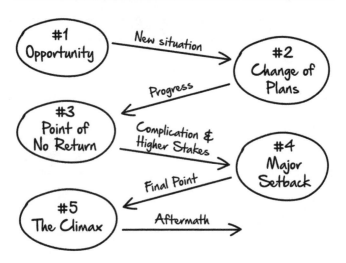

1. **The New Opportunity** After you share the character's backstory, some event causes the character to physically leave where they are and start the journey. This new opportunity is what sets them off to achieve their desires. This leads our hero into a new situation that seems good at first, until they move into turning point #2.

2. **Change of Plans** At some point, the original desire will transform into a very specific, visible goal with a clearly defined end point. This is where the hero's outer motivation is revealed. From here, they will start to make progress toward that goal, until they hit turning point #3.

3. **Point of No Return** At this point, the hero must fully commit to reaching the goal. Up to this point, they've had opportunities to

turn back. But something happens here that makes this a do-or-die situation. It's no longer a should; it's a must. The hero must burn their old bridges and dive in with both feet, or turn back forever. This forces them to start moving into more complicated situations with higher stakes, which lead to turning point #4.

4. **The Major Setback** Something happens to the hero, and we believe that all is lost. This event initially leaves the hero with no chance of success, but then we see a small glimmer of light. The hero has only one option. He has to take one last all-or-nothing shot at the desire. This leads the hero to the final push that drives him to turning point #5.

5. **The Climax** Now our hero must face the biggest obstacle of the entire story and determine their own fate. The journey of achievement will be resolved once and for all, and the journey of transformation will be revealed. Then we move into the aftermath of the story—the hero's new life is revealed, and the journey is complete.

Isn't that cool? Look at almost every successful movie and you will see the pattern of the hero's two journeys.

When I first learned this whole process, I got really excited. And honestly, a little overwhelmed. So I tried to find a way to simplify it, but not lose out on the key elements needed to cause emotion and create an epiphany. And that's when we created these epiphany bridge scripts that I now use dozens of times a day. If you learn nothing else from this book, mastering this process will serve you for the rest of your life in everything you do.

THE EPIPHANY BRIDGE SCRIPT

N ow that you understand the concept of the Epiphany Bridge, and you've also seen the structure of the hero's two journeys, we have everything we need to start creating powerful Epiphany Bridge stories. The Epiphany Bridge script follows a similar path as the hero's two journeys, but I built it in a way that makes telling your stories very simple. I have this on my desk and I use it all

THE EPIPHANY BRIDGE SCRIPT

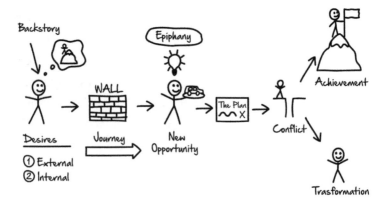

the time when I'm telling my stories. You'll be telling a lot of stories, so mastering this script will become one of the most important things you could ever do. Let me jump in and show you how it works.

An Epiphany Bridge story has eight core sections that pull you through the hero's two journeys. I have a question that goes with each section, and answering each question actually creates the story for me. I will go into more depth for each of the questions below, but let me show you quickly how it works.

1. **The Backstory:** What is your backstory that gives us a vested interest in your journey?
2. **Your Desires:** What is it you want to accomplish?
   a. **External:** What is the external struggle you are dealing with?
   b. **Internal:** What is the internal struggle you are dealing with?
3. **The Wall:** What was the wall or problem you hit within your current opportunity that started you on this new journey?
4. **The Epiphany:** What was the epiphany you experienced and new opportunity you discovered?
5. **The Plan:** What was the plan you created to achieve your desire?
6. **The Conflict:** What conflict did you experience along the way?
7. **The Achievement:** What was your end result?
8. **The Transformation:** What was the transformation you experienced?

For many of you, that outline and those questions will be enough to give you the framework to tell any story. But I wanted to dig a little deeper into each question so you have a really clear understanding on how to answer those questions.

The Backstory
"What is your backstory that gives us a vested interest in your journey?"

Most good stories start with the backstory. For an Epiphany Bridge, that means remembering where you were before you had your big "aha". Go back to that time and place, and remember the circumstances that caused you to start on your hero's journey. Usually this backstory starts at about the same point where your listener is in their life right now.

They desire the same result that you have already achieved. But when they see you as the expert and see what you've accomplished, it can be really hard for them to relate to you and trust you. That's why you must come down from your positioning as an expert, and return to the beginning where you were struggling with the same things they are. When they see that you were once where they are now, they will have faith that you can take them where they want to go.

Your Desires
"What is it you want to accomplish?"

When you created your plot statement, you learned about the three foundational elements of every good story.

- Character
- Desire
- Conflict

Here is where you talk about what it is that you desired the most. What most people miss is that there are almost always two types of struggles keeping you from what you desire the most: the more surface-level external struggles and, more importantly, the deeper internal struggles that you (and your listeners) are experiencing.

"What is the external struggle you are dealing with?"

The external struggle is what drives the journey of accomplishment—the hero's first journey. It's tied to your desire and is usually based on one of the goals you learned about earlier: to win, to retrieve, to escape, or to stop.

People are usually willing to share their external struggles, "I'm trying to lose weight, but I can't give up carbs." Or "I want to start my own company, but I just can't find the time." But these are rarely the real issues they are dealing with. To find out the true cause of their pain, you need to dig deeper and share your internal conflicts.

"What is the internal struggle you are dealing with?"

The internal struggle is the journey of transformation from fear to courage—the hero's second journey. This is the root cause of your struggles.

Sometimes it's hard to share, or even know, what the actual internal struggles are. But if you're willing and able to get vulnerable and share your internal struggles, this will build rapport faster than anything else you can do. Why? Because your audience also shares these same internal struggles. Most people never talk about them, but when they hear you get vulnerable and expose what you are really struggling with, the audience will form an almost instant connection with you.

I've found that the secret to identifying people's internal struggles is to take their external struggle, and ask them "Why?" about five or six times. Keep drilling down until you get to the real reason they want to change. Here's a hint: It's usually tied to love or status—or both.

For example, if someone tells you they want to lose weight, ask them, "Why?"

"Well, because I want to be healthy."

"Why?"

"Because I have three kids, and I want to keep up with them."

"Why?"

"Because by 5:00 p.m., I'm completely out of energy, and I just want to lie down."

"Why?"

"Because I don't want people to think I'm a bad mom."

(Notice that the first few reasons are almost always tied to status.)

"Why?"

"Because I want my kids to know that I love them."

"Why?"

"Because I never knew whether my mom loved me…"

BOOM!

(Notice that this one is tied to love.)

Or if someone wants to make money, ask, "Why?"

"So I can get a bigger house, and my wife can quit her job."

"Why?"

"So that I can provide a better life for my family."

"Why?"

"Because my kids are in daycare, and I really think they should be home with their mom."

"Why?"

"Because my definition of a successful family is having my wife stay home with my kids."

"Why is that important?"

"Because my mom was home when I got home from school, and I want that for my kids, too."

"Why?"

"Because people may think I'm a bad father if I can't provide this way for them."

(Notice status reason here.)

"Why?"

"Because I want my kids to love me and look up to me."

There it is again!

The internal struggle is not that they want to make money, it's that they want their kids and spouse to love them. They want love, security, status.

As you're telling the story, touch upon the external, because that's what they're willing to acknowledge. But then share your internal struggles, too. Those people who are dealing with the same internal struggles will have instant rapport with you, and you'll be speaking to them at a subconscious level. They'll be thinking about feelings they've never really shared in the past, but know are true.

When you get to the end of the story, typically you've solved the external struggles and accomplished what the hero has set out to do. But for your story to be really impactful, the hero needs to have done more than just accomplish their goal. They need to have become someone different in the process.

In fact, sometimes it's even more powerful if the hero does not reach their initial goal. Lightning McQueen didn't win the Piston Cup. Rocky Balboa lost to Apollo Creed (in Part 1), but that is why we love those characters so much. Even though they failed at their external goals, both of them won their internal struggles, the journey of transformation.

Michael Hauge said that the internal journey is all about the death of our identity, and the rebirth of our essence. Our internal struggles are about us holding onto these things that we're attached to such as love, our status, our identity. If you took away all those things, what is left would be your essence. Realizing that your kids love you no matter what, and that others don't really care about your status that much—that is the essence of happiness.

So while we want our hero to achieve his goal, it's more important that he becomes someone different along the way. There has been a death of his internal struggles and a rebirth of something more.

The Wall
"What was the wall or problem you hit within your current opportunity that started you on this new journey?"

The backstory builds rapport with the character, then takes the listener to the moment of frustration that causes our hero to start on their journey. That wall is the frustration you felt because of the current opportunity you have been using to try to accomplish your desires. This old opportunity is not working and is the reason you (as well as your listeners) are willing to go on a journey to try something new.

This is what drives the emotion for the listener and sets up the correct circumstances for them to experience the epiphany. Something happened on your journey that has kept you from your desire. The wall is often a point of frustration, fear, or hopelessness. So be sure to spend time here describing how you felt. This will help to get them into the same state you were in when you had your big epiphany.

The Epiphany
"What was the epiphany you experienced and new opportunity you discovered?"

So far, the hero has been introduced, we know what the ultimate desire is, and we also know the wall their current opportunity has created that is keeping them from their goal. This is the point where something happens that shows them the path they need to follow. It could be a person who helps them understand something. It might be an idea they had while reading, or it could be a breakthrough they discovered while trying to overcome conflict. Something happened that gave them the epiphany, which changed their perception of reality.

Now that you've had this epiphany about what you needed to do, what was the new opportunity it led you to? The epiphany is the thought or the idea, and the new opportunity is the vehicle you've decided to step into to accomplish that goal.

The Plan
"What was the plan you created to achieve your desire?"

Now that you've had the epiphany, and you've learned about the new opportunity, now we talk about the plan you've created to see if this new opportunity will lead you to what you desire the most. What is the plan, and then what are the steps you took to get to your goals?

Inside this plan, you are inevitably going to run into conflict, which is where we start to get the emotion from the story. Remember, it isn't the desire of the character that causes the emotion; it comes from the conflict they experience while they are trying to reach that goal.

The Conflict
"What conflict did you experience along the way?"

After the hero develops a plan, they move forward on it until something happens, they start to run into conflict. We call this the POINT OF NO RETURN because before this point, they could have easily just walked away from the plan and things would have been okay. Here something happens where they must either decide to go back to their old life, or burn the boats and keep moving forward.

This is where you take the step of faith out into the dark, only to find that there's a light just a little further ahead. Most people are so scared of executing on an idea—an "aha", an epiphany—that they never move forward.

In spite of all the reasons you may have said no in the past, this time it's different. This is when the desire shifts from a SHOULD to a MUST. You move from "I should lose weight." to "I MUST lose weight." Or "I should start a business." to "I MUST!"

This will sound like a battle cry to your prospects because they, too, have been "should-ing" for too long. It's time to finally make the change once and for all. They will see you as someone who successfully took a stand and shifted from SHOULD to MUST. And you will inspire them to do the same. Describe for them the moment you made the shift, including how it felt inside.

In all good stories, after the hero has moved past the point of no return, things start to fall apart. They discover the journey isn't as easy as they had assumed in the beginning. If they had known all the pain they'd have to go through, they might never have started the journey at all.

Describe the major setback and conflict you experienced that made you feel like all was lost. But then…there was a glimmer of light, one last way you could accomplish your goal. You alter your plan and go for one last final push.

The Achievement
"What was your end result?"

After your final push, something happens. Either you achieve your external desires, or you don't. Share the aftermath of what happened so people can see the results that you got from the new opportunity.

The Transformation
"What was the transformation you experienced?"

Here you talk about who you became through this process. This is the resolution of your internal struggles, and is the death of the hero's identity and the rebirth of your new belief systems.

As you will see in the next secret, the goal of all good stories is to break old belief patterns and rebuild them with new ones. When you create your stories this way, you are helping people to break free from their old belief systems and create a new future. That is the goal of a good Epiphany Bridge story.

THE EPIPHANY BRIDGE QUESTIONS

That's the script for writing an Epiphany Bridge story. We've covered a lot here, so you could understand the power behind each section of the Epiphany Bridge story. But remember that stories are simple by nature.

THE EPIPHANY BRIDGE QUESTIONS

1. The Backstory: What is your backstory that gives us a vested interest in your journey?
2. Your Desires: What is it that you want to accomplish?
   a. External: What is the external struggle you are dealing with?
   b. Internal: What is the internal struggle you are dealing with?
3. The Wall: What was the wall / problem that you hit within your current opportunity that started you on this new journey?
4. The Epiphany: What was the epiphany you experienced and new opportunity that you discovered?
5. The Plan: What was the plan you created to achieve your desire?
6. The Conflict: What conflict did you experience along the way?
7. The Achievement: What was the end result that you achieved?
8. The Transformation: What was the transformation that you experience?

You can make stories more complex by going deeper into the settings, emotions, other characters, etc. But at their core, they follow a very simple progression.

YOUR ORIGIN EPIPHANY BRIDGE STORY

As I'm sure you can tell so far, each chapter builds on itself, and each secret gives you the next piece you need in the puzzle. So I wanted to step back and talk about a few things, so you can see where your first Epiphany Bridge story fits.

In Secret #5, we talked about the Big Domino, the One Thing you must get them to believe to join your new opportunity.

Here is the Big Domino statement I created for ClickFunnels:

If I can make people believe that <u>funnels</u> are the key to <u>online business success</u> and are only attainable through <u>ClickFunnels</u>, then all other objections and concerns become irrelevant and they have to give me money.

Now obviously I believe that is true, but why? What was the epiphany I had that made that belief become truth for me? That story, the one that made you believe in your domino statement, is what I call the "origin story".

So what I want you to do for this chapter is think about your origin story and then answer the Epiphany Bridge questions. This is the story you will be using often in the sales process, so it's important to take some time and make sure you create it correctly.

As an example, I'll tell you my funnel origin story that I affectionately call the Potato Gun Story.

1. **What is your backstory that gives us a vested interest in your journey?** I was a broke college student athlete trying to make

money online. I learned that people were making money selling information products online, so I created a DVD teaching people how to make potato guns and started to sell it. I was using the extra money I made from our potato gun sales to keep wrestling so I wouldn't have to drop out of school.

2. **What is it you want to accomplish?** I wanted to be able to support my wife so she wouldn't have to work and we could eventually start our family.

   a. **What is the external struggle you are dealing with?** The external struggle was that I was only making a few dollars a day, and many days I actually lost money, so I wasn't able to make enough money to support her, let alone a new baby.

   b. **What is the internal struggle you are dealing with?** The internal struggle was that my wife was supporting me. I was supposed to be the man in the relationship, but my wife was working two jobs while I was going to school, wrestling, and living out my dreams. I felt like a failure as a husband.

3. **What was the wall or problem you hit within your current opportunity that started this new journey?** The problem was that Google had changed their algorithms and increased their ad costs. Suddenly my little potato gun website was no longer making any money, so I had to turn it off, which literally killed my only source of income.

4. **What was the epiphany you experienced and new opportunity you discovered?** I met a friend who told me about how he was adding upsells to his products. By doing that, he was able to make more money from every customer who came in, and therefore all his websites started working again in spite of Google's increased costs. I learned that normal websites weren't enough anymore to make money online, you needed an actual

sales funnel. So I found someone who was selling potato gun kits, and I partnered with them and started selling them as an upsell. After I added a potato gun kit as an upsell for the DVD, I started making money again. I was spending about $10 a day in ads and making $50 or $60 back. That's when I realized that the secret to making money online was creating sales funnels.

5. **What was the plan you created to achieve your desire?** My plan was to start creating sales funnels in other markets that had better potential to make money than the potato gun market. I started creating funnels and selling products in the weight loss market. But we didn't stop there. We then created and started selling supplements to people who suffered from diabetic neuropathy. After that, we created funnels in the couponing, dating, and parenting markets, and others.

6. **What conflict did you experience along the way?** Each new funnel we created took between 6 to 8 weeks to create, on average. We had a team of 8 full-time people including designers, programmers, and copywriters just to get one funnel live. We had to glue together about 13 different products just to create one funnel. On average, our costs to get one funnel live were about $30,000, and then only about 1 out of 10 would actually recoup that money. It took a lot of time and money to find another winning funnel.

7. **What was the end result you achieved?** We ended up getting so frustrated that we decided to create a platform that would make it really easy for us to create sales funnels. The project nickname when we started was "ClickFunnels". We thought if we could build something that would make it possible to build in 1 day what used to take us 6 to 8 weeks, we'd be really happy. After 8 months of programming and every penny I had ever made, we created ClickFunnels. I can now build in an hour—

by myself, without any tech people—what used to take me and my team of 8 guys 6–8 weeks, and these funnels run faster and converted way higher. We then started to let other entrepreneurs use ClickFunnels. Within just 2 years, over 30,000 people use ClickFunnels to power their entire businesses. In fact, in 2016, we had 71 people who made over a million dollars with a single funnel.

8. **What was the transformation you experienced?** After creating ClickFunnels, I was not only able to let my wife become a full-time mom, I've also been able to spend a lot less time working, because we can create things so quickly. I'm now able to be with my kids, and never miss any of the highlights of their lives.

Now that you've read my potato gun epiphany origin story, I want you to re-read my Big Domino statement and see if that story gives you the "aha" you need to be able to believe this statement:

If I can make people believe that <u>funnels</u> are the key to <u>online business success</u> and are only attainable through <u>ClickFunnels</u>, then all other objections and concerns become irrelevant and they have to give me money.

If I did this right, then you should believe that you need a funnel to be successful online, and that the only way to build one is by using ClickFunnels. If you believe that, then your resistance to buying becomes almost zero.

Now that you understand story structure and you've created your first Epiphany Bridge story, in the next section we are going to dig deeper into the false beliefs people have about your new opportunity, and then look at the stories we need to create to break those false belief patterns.

FALSE BELIEF PATTERNS

FALSE BELIEF PATTERNS

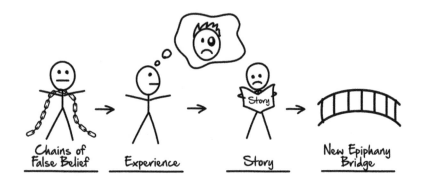

Chains of False Belief — Experience — Story — New Epiphany Bridge

We all create belief systems that support our decisions. We've been doing it pretty much from the day we were born. Those belief systems form the foundations for our lives. We create these beliefs to keep us safe and to safeguard our status. And while they've been developed to protect us, oftentimes they're also the things that keep us from progressing in our lives.

When I'm trying to sell someone on my new opportunity, almost instantly their subconscious mind will start thinking about all the reasons it isn't possible, or why it won't work for them. The bad news is that these beliefs can be really strong.

Let me show you how these beliefs are created. It all starts with an experience. It could be positive or negative, but immediately after they have that experience, their mind quickly creates a story about what that experience meant. Our brain then takes that story we created and it becomes a belief. It's pretty simple, yet that process has happened tens of thousands of times in your life and has created the person you are today.

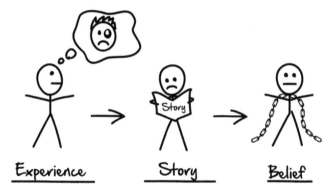

Experience   Story   Belief

It's interesting that two people can have the exact same experience, but because of the story they created, it affected their beliefs about it. So you have to understand that when you speak to people about your new opportunity, they will bring thousands of preconceived beliefs with them that you have to combat if you are going to make the sale.

The good news is that when you know what those false belief patterns are, and you understand the experiences and the stories that your prospects have created in their minds, you can actually use Epiphany Bridge stories to replace their old stories—break their false beliefs—and create new ones.

Here is a fun exercise to demonstrate how this works.

FALSE BELIEF PATTERNS

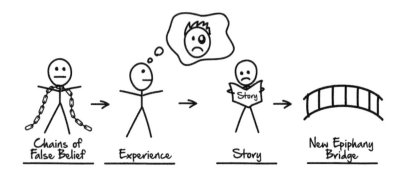

Chains of False Belief   Experience   Story   New Epiphany Bridge

Step #1 What "false chains of belief" might your potential customer have about your new opportunity? For example, if you're in network marketing or multi-level marketing (MLM), a false chain of belief might be something like:

> "If I joined a network marketing / MLM program, I could lose my friends."
> Or if your opportunity is about weight loss:
> "If I try to lose weight, I'm going to be miserable."

If you're not able to think of false beliefs that your potential prospects might have, think about the false beliefs that you had before your big epiphany.

Step #2 Now that you have the false belief, the next step is to figure out what experience they had in their lives that caused the false beliefs. What is the most likely experience your prospect had that caused this belief?

> "One time I joined an MLM, I tried to sign up my parents, and they got mad."

"I tried to lose weight last year, had to cut out carbs, and I was miserable."

Step #3 What is the false story they are telling themselves now that's creating doubt about your new opportunity?

"My story is that people have to bug their friends and family to have success in network marketing."

"My story is that I have to give up things that make me happy if I want to lose weight."

Step #4 Now it's your job to find an Epiphany Bridge story (usually in your own life, but it can also work if you share someone else's story) that shows how you once had a similar belief, but because of this new story, you now have a new belief pattern, and that the old story you were telling yourself was wrong.

"I also thought I had to give up friends if I joined an MLM, but then I learned that you can actually generate leads online. The internet is full of people who want to join my program! So I can grow my team without involving my friends or family."

"I also thought I'd have to give up things that make me happy to lose weight. But then I learned about ketosis and how I can lose weight by drinking ketones instead of cutting carbs."

Isn't that exciting? When I first started to understand this concept, I realized that stories are the keys to belief. If I can identify people's false beliefs and tell stories that show them the truth, I didn't need to "sell" them anything. The stories lead people to the right belief, and they sell themselves.

If you've ever heard me speak, you know I share a lot of stories. In fact, during a recent presentation, one of my friends counted how many stories I told within the first 60 minutes. I had guessed the number might be 10 or so, but the total ended up being over 50—almost one per minute! Some longer stories may take anywhere from 5–10 minutes, while others are often less than a minute.

But the key is I use a lot of stories when I am speaking. They break false beliefs and rebuild the new beliefs people need to make a change. And that is why it's essential for you to start building up your inventory of stories. Here's how you do it.

FALSE BELIEF PATTERNS

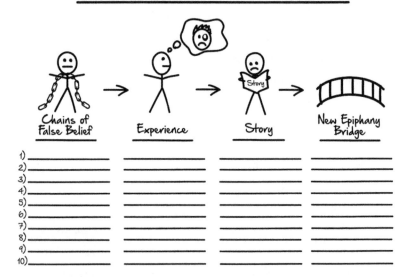

Step #1 List all the false beliefs your customers might have related to your new opportunity. If you struggle trying to figure them out, think about the false beliefs YOU had before you got started on this path. It's likely your audience holds those same beliefs. I try to list at least 10, but normally my list will have 20 or more.

Step #2 What experiences might have caused those false beliefs? List an experience for each false belief on your list.

Step #3 What stories are they telling themselves now because of those experiences? It's important to know their stories, because your new Epiphany Bridge story will replace those old stories.

Step #4 Think about your own Epiphany Bridge story for each of those false beliefs. What happened to change that belief for you? As you build out these steps for your customers, you'll notice that you had mostly the same beliefs, experiences, and stories. So just go back in time and remember what gave you the big "aha" that shattered those beliefs for you. Make sure you have a story for each of the false beliefs. If you don't have a personal story, it's okay to use stories from your customers or even people in the news.

You might not use all these stories, but you should start building up an inventory of stories to use in the future. After you complete all four steps, go back and practice telling your stories using the Epiphany Bridge script from Secret #6. The better you get at telling the stories, the more effective you'll become at persuading others, and you'll know exactly what to say when customers bring up objections.

THE 3 SECRETS

WHAT KEEPS THEM FROM BELIEVING?

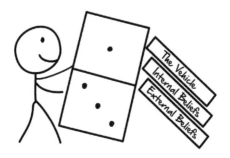

I n a perfect world, you would present someone with your new opportunity, you'd know what the Big Domino was, you'd tell an Epiphany Bridge story to give them a new belief, the Big Domino would fall, and you'd have a customer or follower for life. Sometimes that does happen. One good epiphany story and they're all in. Many times, though, once you change that big belief for them, they immediately start coming up with other concerns. This is especially true with more expensive opportunities and big life changes.

I've found that there are three core beliefs that come to the surface and keep someone from buying, even if they believe the new opportunity is right for them.

1. **The Vehicle:** other false beliefs they may have about the vehicle or new opportunity you're presenting
2. **Internal Beliefs:** beliefs about their own abilities to execute on the new opportunity
3. **External Beliefs:** false beliefs they have about outside forces that could keep them from success; things beyond the individual's control, such as time or the economy

So in a more complicated sale, you need to imagine what their false beliefs are related to each of these three things. The good news is that if you completed the exercise in Secret #9, you already have a huge list. You just need to put each of the false beliefs into the correct categories.

THE CORE FALSE BELIEFS

① The Vehicle ② Internal Beliefs ③ External Beliefs

So all the false beliefs you found that are related to "the vehicle", put them into the first column. False beliefs about their own "internal beliefs" go in the second column, and "external beliefs" into the third. Now decide which of those false beliefs is the CORE belief holding them back in each column and put it at the top.

Go ahead and do this exercise now. You'll be using this information throughout the rest of this book.

Now that you have your list of false beliefs, you will also need an Epiphany Bridge story to go with each of them. You will be using the stories more when we get to Section Three. For now, just create the list and identify the #1 reason in each category that would keep them from taking action on your new opportunity.

Let me show you an example.

In my ClickFunnels presentation, I initially pique their curiosity by sharing my opportunity switch headline we created in Secret #4:

How to Create a 7-Figure Funnel in Less Than 30 Minutes Without Having to Hire, or Be Held Hostage by, a Tech Guy

Then my goal is to get them to believe in the Big Domino statement I created in Secret #5:

If I can make people believe that <u>funnels</u> are the key to <u>online business success</u> and are only attainable through <u>ClickFunnels</u>, then all other objections and concerns become irrelevant and they have to give me money.

Then I tell them my potato gun Epiphany Bridge story from Secret #8 so they have the first "aha" that they need to have a funnel, too. But as soon as I do that, the core false beliefs about the Big Domino rise to the surface.

False Belief #1 (The Vehicle) "Funnels sound cool, but I don't understand how they would work for me."

False Belief #2 (Internal Beliefs) "I'm sold on funnels, but I'm not technically inclined, so I don't think I could build one."

False Belief #3 (External Beliefs) "I think I could build a funnel, but even if I did, I don't know how to drive traffic into it."

Now that I have the three core false beliefs, I have to find the Epiphany Bridge stories that will break them.

False Belief #1: I don't understand how it would work for me.

- **Epiphany Bridge Stories for False Belief #1:** For this, I tell them my Tony Robbins and Porter Stansberry stories showing them about modeling success, as well as my Funnel Hacking story about how we modeled the Marine-D3 funnel to build our Neuracel funnel and how they can do that with any successful funnel in their market.

False Belief #2: I'm not technical.

- **Epiphany Bridge Stories for False Belief #2:** I tell the story about how I used to have a big tech team build funnels that cost thousands of dollars, and how we were able to change that after we built ClickFunnels. I then show them a product demo so they see how easy it is even if they are not technical.

False Belief #3: I don't know how to drive traffic.

- **Epiphany Bridge Stories for False Belief #3:** I tell them my story about how I reverse engineer from where my competitors get traffic, so I can easily get traffic from the same places.

So I am plugging in my Epiphany Bridge stories that I created in Secret #9 that will break their core chains of false belief.

Finally, I rewrite each of those false beliefs and the stories that go with them into a "secret" that causes curiosity so people will want to listen. Curiosity is the key!

Here is how I rewrote my three core false beliefs into my three secrets.

Secret #1: Funnel Hacking How to Ethically Steal Over $1,000,000 Worth of Funnel Hacks from Your Competitors for Under $100

Secret #2: Funnel Cloning How to Clone a PROVEN Funnel (Inside of ClickFunnels) in Less Than 10 Minutes

Secret #3: My #1 Traffic Hack How to Get the Exact SAME Customers Who Are Currently Going to Your Competitors to Start Coming to Your Funnel Instead!

The 3 Secrets Of Funnel Hacking...

- Secret #1: Funnel Hacking:
  "How To Ethically Steal Over $1,000,000 Of 'Funnel Hacks' From Your Competitors, For Under $100"
- Secret #2: Funnel Cloning:
  "How To Then Clone Their PROVEN Funnel (In Click Funnels) In Less Than 10 Minutes..."
- Secret #3: My #1 Traffic Hack:
  "How To Get The Exact SAME Customers Who Are Currently Going To Your Competitors Funnels... To Start Coming To YOUR Funnel Instead!"

click funnels   #funnelhacker

Now that you have all these elements, you have the foundation you need to start creating your sales presentation in Section Three. You will be plugging these three secrets into a slide that looks similar to the image on page 138.

Do you see the power behind what you've created here?

You've identified the one Big Domino that will get people to believe in your message, as well as the three core false beliefs that are holding that domino up. In the presentation you will be creating in the next chapter, you'll use stories to systematically knock down each of the beliefs holding up the Big Domino.

When all three of the core false beliefs have been knocked down, the Big Domino tumbles. When that happens, you have introduced the belief necessary for them to take action. It's all about breaking the false belief patterns holding your prospects back and rebuilding true beliefs.

In Section Three, I'll show you how to take these conceptual strategies and create the tactical pieces you need to make the sale.

SECTION THREE

YOUR MORAL OBLIGATION

Section One was all about creating your own mass movement. In Section Two, you learned more about how to build up your followers' beliefs so you can introduce them to new opportunities that will change their lives. In this section, we'll shift gears and talk about sales.

One of my mentors, Jay Abraham, said that "if you believe in the product or service you're selling, then you have a moral obligation to try and serve your customers in every way possible."

Often we make the mistake of thinking that because our content is so good, people will automatically follow us and pay for that information. Unfortunately, that just isn't true. One great example of this is Inner Circle member, Justin Williams. His company flips more than 100 houses per year, netting over a million dollars. And the best part is he does it all in under five hours per week.

So Justin decided to take his expertise, create a course, and sell it. His story and the proof he had was amazing. Yet even though he tried selling it for over a year, almost no one bought the course. He was shocked, because this had changed his life and he knew it would for other people, too. He couldn't figure out why no one would buy it. Then he and his wife, Tara, decided to join my Inner Circle to learn how to sell their program. By mastering the strategies in this section, they took this little coaching company they had almost shut down to over a million dollars within just eight months.

The term "sales" sometimes has a negative connotation. But when you layer sales on top of the strategies I've already shown you, this process becomes simple. I'm going to show you how to take the new opportunity and stories you've created and weave them into a presentation that will convert your listeners into customers.

The script you will learn over the next 6 secrets took me over 10 years to create and master. It's now been used by hundreds of entrepreneurs just like you to sell large groups of people products and services in the shortest amount of time possible.

I still remember the first time I saw somebody sell a product onstage. They did a 90-minute presentation teaching about a concept, and then at the end they made the crowd a special offer. I watched in amazement as hundreds of people ran to the back of the room and gave this person thousands of dollars! It was so exciting and, as I was counting how many people signed up and multiplying it by his program fee, I realized that he had made over $100,000 in just 90 minutes! I knew at that moment that I HAD to master that skill.

So at my very first speaking engagement, I prepared a presentation that I knew was going to be amazing and would cause people to run to the back and sign up for my new program just like I had seen others do before me. I finally got on stage, nervously gave my presentation, and made a special offer at the end. But what happened next was shocking to me.

Crickets. No…body…moved. No one bought anything. It was so humiliating, I spent the rest of the weekend in my hotel room hiding and eating Haagen-Dazs and coconut shrimp and watching movies, because I couldn't face the other speakers or attendees. It was a total bomb!

I was so embarrassed, I swore I'd never speak or sell from the stage again. I was going to sit behind my computer and just sell things online. But I discovered that the skills I needed to sell online were the same skills I was lacking when I spoke from the stage. So I decided to humble myself and learn. I didn't want to learn from people who were good speakers, but rather from people who could actually SELL from their respective platforms (such as stage, teleseminars, webinars). There's a HUGE difference between the two.

What I discovered from the best people in the business was that teaching the best content actually hurt sales. But learning how to identify, break, and rebuild false belief patterns got people to take the action they needed in order to change. I learned how to tell stories. I learned how to structure offers and so much more. Then, for three years, I stood on stages all around the world, in front of thousands of people, and tested the presentations over and over and over again. I watched closely to see which topics (in what order) would make people run to the back of the room with their credit cards in hand. I also paid attention to what slowed my sales.

Then one day I decided I was tired of traveling and leaving my family behind. So I quit speaking from the stage, despite the fact that I could bring in $250,000 or more from a single 90-minute presentation. Instead I transferred those selling skills to the online environment. I tested my script on teleseminars, and then webinars. I used it for video sales letters, Facebook Live presentations, and more.

Each time I presented using this script, I'd watch the response and make tweaks. I did it over and over again, for years. A few years ago, I started teaching this script and process to my Inner Circle members.

They implemented the script in all sorts of different markets. Dozens of them have now become millionaires, using this exact same script.

It works...

It's perfect...

It's worth mastering if you really want to get your message to your market.

THE STACK SLIDE

B efore I ever start selling anything, my first step is to create an irresistible offer. This is the product I am selling at the end of my presentation. I do that with something I call the "stack slide". This is where I stack up everything a customer gets when they decide to buy, including all the bonuses and extras.

THE STACK SLIDE

What You're Gonna Get...

Masterclass	($9,997 value)
Tools	($997 value)
Tangible #1	($297 value)
Tangible #2	($297 value)
Tangible #3	($297 value)
Bonus	(Priceless)

Total value: $11,885

To start this process, I normally stand in front of a white board and write down everything I could create for my dream customer to get them their desired result. I spend a few hours brainstorming everything I can think up—from providing a cool template to speed up their success to flying to their house and helping them in person! After my initial brain dump, I sit down and create the stack slide. I add in the coolest ideas from the white board that I'd be willing to deliver for the price I have in mind.

Every item on the stack slide has a value attached to it. The goal is to show that you're giving 10 times as much value as you're asking for in price. So if you're selling a $97 product, you want the stack slide to add up to at least $997, preferably more. If you're selling a product for $997, then the value needs to be at least $9,997.

Some people get concerned about assigning a value to each of the offer components. Think of it not as the value you'd sell it for, but the value they get from it. What will the results from each element be worth to them?

Over the years, I've developed six types of elements that work best in my offers.

Element #1: The Opportunity Switch Masterclass The first thing to include on your stack slide is the actual system that teaches them the new opportunity. This is what you will teach your beta group during your free masterclass. After you teach it once for free, it will be fleshed out in more detail in the actual course you'll be selling, or it could just end up being the recordings from your beta masterclass.

Element #2: The Tools As someone participates in your masterclass, what are some tools you can give them to make the process easier for them and help them succeed? A tool can be something complex, such as software (one of the best tools), or something more simple, such as a template they need to fill in or checklists to follow.

One of my Inner Circle members, Liz Benny, sells a masterclass for people who want to become social media managers. She gives away all her contracts, so her students don't have to hire expensive lawyers or come up with their own. While they certainly could draft their own, and she could teach them how to do that in the training, it's more valuable to just have them already done.

Basically, she's selling a by-product of her own business. She's already created the contracts for herself, so it's no extra work to offer them to others who are learning the same process. What by-products have you created that you could offer your customers?

Extra training is rarely a good stack item because most people assume that more training equals more work. People want tangible assets that make the core training easier to implement. Scripts, templates, cheat sheets, checklists, timelines, and schedules are all valuable tools you could create. Tools often have a much higher perceived value than the actual masterclass they paid for, so it's worth investing some time to make something awesome.

Element #3: Tangible #1 (Related to the Vehicle) What false beliefs do your customers have about the vehicle / new opportunity that you're presenting to them? What would keep them from believing that this vehicle is right for them? What tangible thing can you create to help them change their belief?

I love creating case studies or examples to include as this bonus. If I were creating a product about flipping houses on eBay, I'd go and find 20–30 examples of me doing this process, or case studies of my students having success with it. I'd put them together into a case study booklet or video training that people could watch or read as proof that the vehicle works and to get a better insight about how others are doing it. The more belief in the new opportunity I can create, the more likely they will be able to achieve the same results.

Element #4: Tangible #2 (Related to Their Internal Struggle)
Once they believe the vehicle is right for them, what beliefs do they
have about THEMSELVES that make them think they can't succeed?
For example, someone in your beta group might say, "That's cool, but
I don't know how to _____." Or "I can't _____." They
might believe in the new vehicle, but they don't believe in themselves.
So you need to create something specific to help them overcome these
false beliefs about themselves.

Maybe they think they're not technically inclined. What can you
create to show them how to hire the right tech people? Maybe they
believe they've never been able to stick to a diet. What tangible can you
create that will help them overcome this internal struggle? Sometimes
this element will be specific training that goes beyond what's in the
masterclass. It could also be tangible tools or templates that will give
them the confidence to realize they can actually do it.

One of my best-selling offers (my Funnel Hacking offer) taught
people how to build funnels. While it was easy to get people to believe
that funnels were the future, they often didn't believe that THEY could
actually build a successful sales funnel on their own. I discovered that
one of their biggest fears was writing the copy for the funnel pages.
So for this element, I gave people my copywriting course, as well as
all my templates and swipe files, so they can easily complete that part
of the process.

Element #5: Tangible #3 (Related to an External Struggle) This
is usually the last thing holding someone back from getting results. They
believe that the vehicle is right, they believe they can do it, but there is
still some outside force that might make it difficult for them to succeed.
This outside force might be a bad economy, lack of time, or something
else outside their direct control.

For my Funnel Hacking offer, getting traffic was the big external
struggle everyone had. They believed in the vehicle, they believed

in themselves, but had fears that no one would ever click into their funnels. So we created a video course showing them how to drive traffic into their funnels.

For your opportunity, think about what outside things might possibly keep people from success, then create something to help eliminate or minimize that excuse.

Element #6: Exclusive Bonus Finally, we need to create something that will cause urgency and scarcity. In my ClickFunnels presentation, I offer an upgraded account for those who sign up before a certain deadline. In my high-ticket secrets course, I give the first 10 people a consult call with one of my sales guys. You can also give them personal access to you via an accountability group, a phone consultation, or a mastermind event.

Here is an example of my stack slide that you can model:

What You're Gonna Get. . .

- **6 Weeks Funnel Hacks Masterclass** ($2,997 Value)
- **ClickFunnels: 6 Month Enterprise Account** ($3,564 Value)
- **Instant Traffic Hacks** ($1,997 Value)
- **Inception Secrets** ($1,997 Value)
- **Soap / Seinfeld Secrets** ($997 Value)
- **Unlimited Funnels In Your Account (First 50 Only)** (Priceless!)

Total Value: $11,552

click funnels   #funnelhacker

Once you have your stack slide assembled, you've got an irresistible offer—a vehicle for real change. In the next secret, you'll learn the script used to present and sell this offer.

THE PERFECT WEBINAR

PERFECT WEBINAR

Intro/Rapport

CONTENT

The ONE Thing

Justify Failures
Encourage Dreams
Allay Fears
Confirm Suspicions
Throw Rocks At Enemies

Secret #1 The Vehicle
Secret #2 Internal Beliefs
Secret #3 External Beliefs

Break and Rebuild Their Belief Patterns

LET ME ASK YOU A QUESTION

CLOSES STACK

Money Is Good	Disposable Income	Money Replenishes	Break Old Habits
Information Alone?	Money or Excuses?	Your 2 Choices	Their 2 Choices
Us VS Them	The Hand Hold	Say Goodbye	Now & Later
Only Excuses	Reluctant Hero	If You Only Got	Close Close

hesitated to call this secret the "Perfect Webinar" because I don't want you to think this script only works for webinars. It was initially created for webinars under that name. But since then, we've successfully used it for video sales letters, teleseminars, webinars, stage presentations, email sequences, and more. It should probably be titled the "Perfect Presentation", but our community has adopted the name the "Perfect Webinar", so we'll keep it the same. Just don't forget that this script can and should be used in all selling situations, not just webinars.

In this secret, I'll break down the script process, then in the next three secrets we'll walk through it step-by-step. Everything covered so far will be plugged into specific sections of the script. (Yes, there is a method to my madness.) And while it may seem like we're doing a lot in this script, there is just one goal.

Get them to believe One Thing.

That's it. If you ask someone to believe in more than one thing, your sales will suffer.

Jason Fladlien once explained:

The idea is to have a **single point of belief** that your message is built around and is emphasized over and over and over again from a variety of different angles.

The Big Domino I mentioned earlier—THAT is the key thing they need to believe. The whole presentation is created to knock down that one domino, and that's it. The three secrets you're about to learn are not NEW things you're trying to get them to believe. They are the tools you use to attack the domino from a variety of different angles. That is the key to the Perfect Webinar. When you understand this, you're ready to build out your presentation.

There are a lot of moving pieces in this script, and every single one of them is there for a specific reason. Make sure you don't leave anything out. Before we dive into each individual element, let's look at an overview of the whole process. There are four major parts.

Part 1: The Introduction / Building Rapport This is where you'll welcome people to the presentation, build rapport, pique their curiosity, and get them excited. Also, this is where you start actually persuading people. That doesn't begin at the close, that begins the second you start talking.

Part 2: The One Thing During this section, you'll try to pique their curiosity, you'll identify the Big Domino (the One Thing), and

tell your first Epiphany Bridge story (your origin story). Right off the bat, you're giving people the same epiphany you had when you discovered the new opportunity. This is your first attempt to knock down the Big Domino.

Part 3: The Three Secrets (Breaking and Rebuilding Belief Patterns) This is the content section of the presentation. You need to identify the false beliefs they have around the following:

1. The vehicle or new opportunity
2. Their ability to use the vehicle (internal beliefs)
3. The #1 thing they believe is keeping them from getting started (external beliefs)

You already identified these earlier, so all you have to do is tell Epiphany Bridge stories that break their false belief systems and rebuild them with the truth.

THE 3 SECRETS

Notice that the three secrets are not trying to get people to believe NEW things. They are simply false beliefs they already have about your One Thing. If you knock down these three beliefs through the content section of the presentation, the Big Domino will fall and they will join your new opportunity.

WHAT KEEPS THEM FROM BELIEVING?

Part 4: The Stack Here is where you move from the teaching to the sales portion of the presentation. (Don't worry if you're nervous about this. I'm going to give you a magic sentence that will make the transition seamless and natural.) You'll then present your offer in a very precise format we call the stack, and you'll weave in some very specific closes that have been proven to persuade people to take the action they need in order to get results. And yes, you will be using your stack slide during this portion of the presentation.

That is the bird's-eye view of the Perfect Webinar structure. After you master it, you'll be able to give a presentation like this on the fly. But it's important to really understand the objectives for each section. So the next three chapters will break down each part of the Perfect Webinar slide by slide.

THE ONE THING

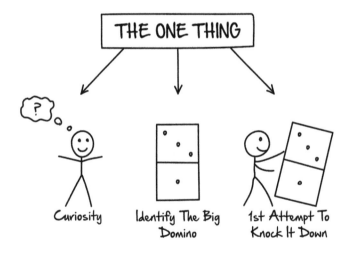

t's time. Are you ready to put your Perfect Webinar presentation script together? You have all the foundational pieces you need at this point. So we're just going to go right through the script writing process from start to finish. You're going to write a whole presentation right now.

Typically, I create this either in PowerPoint or Keynote, so I'm going to teach the next few sessions slide by slide with an image to show the concept behind each one. If you're doing a webinar, this graphic shows what you'd put on the slides. If you're using this script as an email sequence or some other selling system, use the slides as a reminder of what you need to cover at each phase.

Let's talk about scripting for a minute. When it comes to presenting webinars, there are two kinds of people. Some like to just look at bullet points on the slide and improvise. And others like to have an entire script written out that they can just read word for word. Personally, I'm in the first group. However, the reason we call this the Perfect Webinar is because we've tightly engineered it to deliver the most conversions. I believe it's as perfect as you can get.

So for right now, I strongly recommend that you script out everything you're going to say word for word. That way, you know you won't forget anything. Once you've delivered the webinar live a few dozen times, it will become second nature and you can improvise all you want. And even if you say, "No way, I don't want to read a script!", at least go through the process of writing it down as you go through this section. I really want you to be successful right out of the gate. Let's go!

THE INTRODUCTION AND THE ONE THING

In a traditional webinar, this first part of the presentation should take 5 to 10 minutes. If you are using this in other selling environments, you can do this part in a much shorter window. Its job is to build rapport and get people excited about what they are going to learn.

1. Title Slide

The title slide is the first thing people will see when they log on to the webinar or watch the replay. It's got the webinar headline you wrote earlier: How to _____ without _____. The goal here is to encourage curiosity and get people to stick around.

> Hey everybody! Welcome to the webinar. This is _____ and today I'm going to show you how to _____ without _____.

This is an example of my title slide:

2. Intro / Rapport

Earlier you learned about *One Sentence Persuasion* by Blair Warren. Remember he said, "People will do anything for those who encourage their dreams, justify their failures, allay their fears, confirm their suspicions, and help them throw rocks at their enemies." I like to cover this at the very beginning of my presentations as a way to build instant rapport with my audience. Here's how we do it.

Justify their failures. "Now I'm guessing for a lot of you this is probably not your first webinar. The first thing I want to mention is that if you've failed at _____ in the past, it's not your fault. There's a lot of information out there, and it can be confusing. Many times that information overload keeps you from success. It's okay."

Allay their fears. "If you've been concerned in the past that you just can't succeed with _____, I want to put those fears to rest. You can do this. You just need the right person to explain it to you."

Throw rocks at their enemies. "The big corporations want you to think you need a lot of venture capital or some fancy college degree to be successful. I'm here to tell you they're wrong. They have their own reasons for wanting you to think that, but it's not true."

Confirm suspicions. "If you've ever thought that the government and the banks actually want you to fail, you're probably right. They don't benefit from you succeeding. They want to keep you in debt and in need. The difference with us is that we actually care about your success and truly want to see you living the life of your dreams."

Encourage their dreams. "So that's what we're here for. I know you have a dream to change the world and make an impact, and I want to show you how to make that happen during this webinar."

3. The Ruler: Goal #1—The New Opportunity (Make It Inclusive)

The next slide is what I call the "ruler." It's the measuring stick people will use to judge your webinar. If you don't tell them what your goals are, even if you do everything perfectly, they may be upset because their goal was different than yours. So I like to tell people right away what my goals are, what I want them to get from the presentation. If they aren't looking for a similar goal, they have the opportunity to leave at that point.

The goal is always to help them to see that this new opportunity will give them their greatest desires, increase their status, and help them achieve their goals.

I also take this opportunity to be inclusive of any people who aren't sure whether they are in the right spot. I don't want people wondering during the whole presentation "Is this for me?" I want them to know up front that this is exactly what they need.

> My goal for this presentation is to help two types of people. For those who are beginners, you'll get [*what the presentation / new opportunity will do for them, or how it will fulfill their desires*]. For more experienced people, you'll get [*alternative*].

Sometimes my inclusion is for beginners versus advanced, but other times it's based on different parts of the market who may be watching. For example:

If you own a retail store, you'll get _____ from my presentation, but if you own an online store, you'll get _____ from the presentation.

4. The Ruler: Goal #2—The Big Domino

This next slide is typically an extension of my goal, and it's where I first show them the Big Domino. Remember you created your Big Domino sentence earlier? It looked like this:

If I can make them believe that [*new opportunity*] is key to [*what they desire most*], and / but it is only attainable through [*specific vehicle*], then all other objections and concerns become obsolete.

So this slide restates that sentence in the form of goals.

My Goal From This Webclass...

1. The ONLY WAY for you to exponentially grow your company is through **Sales Funnels...**
2. The ONLY WAY to build funnels, is through **ClickFunnels**.

click funnels   #funnelhacker

Remember, they need to believe that your specific vehicle is the ONLY way to get what they desire most.

5. Qualify Yourself

Here is where you introduce yourself and let people know why they should listen to you. I'm not a big fan of bragging, but you need to

make sure you have postured yourself in a way that they see you as an expert and an authority. This shows them you have already achieved what they desire.

Don't get into the game of sharing every stat about yourself and reading a 10-page bio. This is annoying and does not build rapport. Briefly touch on the external result, but then dig a little deeper and talk about the internal result your achievement gave you as well. These are the two things you'll be discussing with your first Epiphany Bridge story.

6. Epiphany Bridge Story #1 (Origin Story)

This is where you transition into your backstory for your first Epiphany Bridge story. Tell your origin story, the series of events that first convinced you this new opportunity was the vehicle for you. This will be your first attempt to knock down the Big Domino. Use the Epiphany Bridge script to tell the story in a way that gives them the same epiphany you had. If you succeed, they will be sold after this first story. And everything else you say from this point forward will strengthen their initial "aha".

7. Liken Your Story to Them

After you tell your epiphany story, some people will think, "That's great, but it has nothing to do with me." So next you need to make it relevant for them. The way you do that is to reframe it in some way that's familiar to their situation. Tell them what's traditionally been done. Then explain why that's hard or confusing. Finally, explain how your solution makes it easy or better.

> You guys probably don't want to be in the potato gun business, but funnels still apply to whatever you do. Here's how you traditionally sell your products—you put a whole bunch of products on a web page and hope visitors buy something before they leave. Here's why that's hard—you have no control over where they're clicking or what they're seeing next. It's just a big hodgepodge of products.
>
> Funnels make e-commerce scalable, because you're leading the customer down a path where they only have to look at one product at a time. And the upsells help you earn more from each customer.

8. Case Study / Proof

If you have a quick case study of someone you've worked with having success with this, or an example that helps them see how it will work for them, you would include that here.

> Not only has this worked for me, but here is a story about Trey, who was on this same webinar recently, and look at the transformation he's had in just 6 short months!

9. Transition to the 3 Secrets

For many people, the initial story will get them excited, but objections and false beliefs will also start to pop up as soon as you introduce the new opportunity. This is where you transition to the content section of the webinar, where you will start breaking and rebuilding their false belief patterns.

Introduce what you're going to teach during the webinar. The 3 Secrets, of course, are designed to counteract or negate the top three false beliefs you just mentioned. You already created the titles of these 3 Secrets, so you can plug them in here and introduce them to everyone.

Here's what we're going to cover during the next 45 minutes or so.

Secret #1: Funnel Hacking > How to Ethically Steal Over $1,000,000 Worth Of Funnel Hacks From Your Competitors For Under $100

Secret #2: Funnel Cloning > How to Then Clone Their PROVEN Funnel (Inside of ClickFunnels) in Less Than 10 Minutes

Secret #3: My #1 Traffic Hack > How to Get The Exact SAME Customers Who Are Currently Going to Your Competitors' Funnels…To Start Coming To Your Funnel Instead!

Okay, now you've got the first part of the presentation scripted. Next, let's dive into the actual content delivery.

BREAKING AND REBUILDING BELIEF PATTERNS

HOW TO BREAK AND REBUILD BELIEF PATTERNS

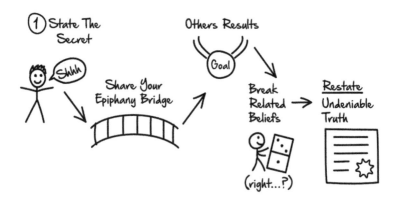

E verything you have done to this point has been designed to encourage curiosity, build rapport, and introduce the new opportunity. Now we're transitioning to the content section of the presentation. You'll be tempted to switch into teacher mode at this point. And if you're not careful, it will destroy your sales.

This is not a teaching presentation; this is a presentation to inspire people and cause them to actually take action to change their lives. The teaching is what you do AFTER they have purchased. Teaching does not have a place in the webinar. It's the surest way to kill sales. Remember, you are focusing on identifying their false belief patterns, breaking them, and rebuilding them with the truth.

I'm sure that for some of you this concept doesn't make sense or you got a little upset about it. When I first tried to sell something I had created that I knew would change people's lives, I did it in teacher mode. I taught my best stuff, knowing that as soon as they heard it, they'd want more. Right? Wrong.

Instead, people told me my content was amazing, but then they just left with all the cool new stuff they had learned. They never actually implemented what I had created for them. While I was trying my best to help them, it actually hurt them because they didn't shift their beliefs, didn't buy anything, and never changed their lives. I was a failed expert and coach. I honestly believe that the greatest service you can provide for someone is getting them to buy something. The act of buying creates a commitment that causes them to actually take action.

Dozens of my friends have come to my events as free guests, where someone sitting next to them had paid $25k to be in the same room. The strange thing is that so far none of those friends have ever actually launched successful businesses from the info they got at the event. None. Yet for those who paid to be in the room, our success rate is almost 100%.

One of my early mentors, Bill Glazer, explained that I was actually keeping people from success because I was teaching them. I was SO confused, and it took me a few years before I understood what he meant and how to change my method so it worked.

Over the years, I slowly learned how to structure my content in such a way that it teaches and inspires, but also (and most importantly) causes people to take action. For some of you, this will feel strange at first because you aren't teaching them all the cool stuff you want to share. But you need to understand that the type of teaching you are doing here is the foundation for change.

I remember being frustrated the first time I did a presentation this way, but when I was done, two very distinct things happened. Instead of making just a few sales like I normally did, I made hundreds of sales. And second, 10 times more people than usual told me that the content changed their lives.

It's kind of funny. Even though I wasn't "teaching" them, I was breaking beliefs that had held them back for years and giving them new, empowering beliefs. This is actually teaching in its most pure form, it's just different than what you're used to. The time for teaching strategy and tactics will come. But they need to come in with the right belief systems first.

10. State the Secret

Here you quickly state the first secret.

Secret #1: How to Ethically Steal Over $1,000,000 Worth of Funnel Hacks From Your Competitors For Under $100

Then you transition immediately into the next slide by saying, "Now let me tell you a quick story…"

11. Share Your Epiphany Bridge

Next, you will tell your second Epiphany Bridge story, which will kill the #1 false belief they have about the new opportunity you are presenting. This story will help the audience better understand the new opportunity. Remember, the goal isn't to teach them, but to tell the stories around it to give them the epiphanies that will create desire and belief. They have to figure it out themselves.

12. Show Other People's Results

The audience will immediately think, *That's great for Russell, but he's like a superhero!* You've already positioned yourself as an expert, as someone successful. So you show some results that ordinary people have gotten from your vehicle. Go back to your initial beta group and start sharing some of those great results, testimonials, and stories that are tied to this first secret.

> The cool thing is it didn't just work for me, it works for all kinds of people. Look, here's Joe, and he always thought _____ was true, but after he took that leap of faith and tried things this way, this is what happened...

13. Break the Related Beliefs

Of course, people are going to have lots of other false beliefs and objections about this secret, right? We made a list of all their false chains of belief in Secret #9, then you listed each one that was related to it in Secret #10. So it's time to revisit the rest of your list from earlier. It's time to break any other core beliefs they might have related to the vehicle.

I learned a cool way to do this from Jason Fladlien. We were doing a webinar and he kept track of every objection he could think of during the whole thing. Then at the end, he spent about 90 minutes busting every objection on the list. He'd say, "You're probably thinking _____, right? Well, _____."

You're probably thinking you need a lot of money to drive traffic, right?

Well actually, you only need 100 clicks a day.

You're probably thinking you need to know how to code, right?

Well actually, you can just clone other people's funnels right inside ClickFunnels.

He went on and on like that for about 50 false beliefs that I hadn't even mentioned in the main webinar. I was starting to sweat because we'd been on for three hours and he was still talking. What were people going to think? But what actually happened was amazing.

At the end of the webinar, we sold three times more during his 90 minutes of "You're probably thinking X, right?" than we sold in the first 90 minutes of the webinar. We were live for three hours and had a record-breaking day. He just kept breaking false beliefs until there were no more objections that anyone could possibly think of. There was absolutely no resistance left.

And it didn't just work that one time. Our Inner Circle clients Brandon and Kaelin Poulin were already killing it on their webinars, selling around $200,000 a month. Then they heard me mention this strategy and tried it out. At the end of their webinar, they went on for 30 minutes just busting through false beliefs, and ended up doubling their sales!

So go back to your lists of false beliefs you created in Secret #9, find the ones associated with this secret, and quickly break those beliefs that may be holding your followers back. These stories are usually told in 30–60 seconds. Just mention the false belief and give a quick story or one or two sentences about why that belief is wrong and what the truth is.

14. Restate the New Belief as an Undeniable Truth

Finally, you're just going to restate the secret as an undeniable truth. The old belief pattern has been shattered, and you've installed a new one. And that's the most powerful thing you can do as an educator and an expert.

So now I've shown you how you can ethically steal over a million dollars' worth of Funnel Hacks for under $100. Isn't that awesome?

15.–24. Rinse and Repeat for Secrets #2 and #3

Once you've gone through these steps for the first secret, go back and repeat steps 10 through 14 for the other two secrets. That's going to be the majority of your webinar content.

When you change your presentation to this style, you are giving them more than just strategies and tactics. You're giving them a paradigm shift. You're changing their world from I CAN'T to I CAN and I WILL. That's the biggest gift you can give people—hope and belief in themselves. When you go through this process, you'll spend 45 to 60 minutes breaking those underlying issues and, all of a sudden, the huge domino falls down. They have a new belief in the One Thing, and the whole world is open to them.

After the webinar, you'll hear people saying, "I learned so much in that webinar. I had this emotional change." Again, you as the educator might feel like you didn't teach that much. But you did more than teach. You completely transformed the way they view the world, which is what you need to do if you're expecting them to adopt your new opportunity.

25. The Transition to Selling

As I start to move from the content section to the stack and closes, I use a few techniques to cement the new concepts into their minds and make a simple, non-stressful transition to the selling section of the presentation.

The first thing is to show them how they could actually get the results they desire most, if they actually follow what I showed them. So I'll go back through my 3 Secrets and say something like:

> So let me ask you a question. If you followed what I showed you in Secret #1 and found a funnel that is already working, then you did what I showed you in Secret #2 and used ClickFunnels to build out a similar funnel in just 10 minutes, and then you used Secret #3 to get traffic from the SAME place your competitors are getting it from, do you think you could be successful?

When you break it down like that so they can connect the dots, they have to say yes. If they've said yes to that question, that means all the internal beliefs have been knocked down, and the Big Domino has fallen.

When I'm speaking onstage and can actually see the audience, those who are nodding their heads to that question are the ones who end up running to the back of the room to buy. If anyone isn't nodding, something in my presentation didn't convince them the Big Domino was true.

When you sell in person, you have the ability to ask follow-up questions and figure out their specific false beliefs. Then you can address those concerns and close them. You don't have that luxury in group sales like webinars. So you have to include as many objections and false beliefs in the presentation as possible.

That first transition question will help you gauge whether they are sold. And it will help them convince themselves that they are sold, as well.

26. The Question

Now it's time to start the actual sales section of the webinar. You've taught the 3 Secrets. You've broken false beliefs. It's time to reveal what you have to offer. The hardest part of selling on a webinar for most people is transitioning into the close. They get nervous and shaky—the hesitation and lack of confidence shows in their voice and body language. I used to get nervous too, until I learned a magic question from one of my mentors, Armand Morin. He taught me that the best way to make that transition is to simply say:

Let me ask you a question…

That's the secret. It takes off all pressure and lets you make a seamless transition.

I then ask them a few things.

How many of you are excited about what we just talked about?!
How many of you are feeling a little overwhelmed because we've covered so much?

Then I try to get them to laugh by showing them a picture of someone with a fire hose in their mouth. That usually gets a laugh, and it allows me to explain how it's impossible to show them everything they need to get results in a 60-minute presentation, but that I tried to cover as much as possible. I tell them that I created a special package for those who are ready to move forward and want to implement this new opportunity.

Then I ASK PERMISSION to share it with them.

> Is it okay with you if I spend 10 minutes going over a very special offer I created to help you implement _____?

Then I wait until they say yes or I see heads nodding. I want them to say yes first. Once you get permission, all the awkward feelings about selling disappear.

In the rare times when no one speaks or there is an awkward silence, I say something like:

> All right, it's totally fine if you guys don't want to know this stuff. I already know it. This isn't about me; this is for you. Are you okay if I spend 10 minutes and show you how it can change your life?

If you've followed the script up to this point, they're going to say yes and you can introduce your offer. This transition helps you recap everything you've said in the webinar up to that point, and once again sets those new belief patterns in place. Once you transition into your sales pitch, you're going to use one of my favorite techniques—the stack.

SECRET #15

THE STACK

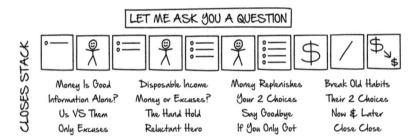

consider this my secret weapon. I learned it after watching Armand Morin speak onstage in front of over 1,000 people. He closed nearly half the room with almost no effort. I pulled him aside to find out what he was doing, and he explained the stack. I started using it immediately and went from closing an average 5–10% of a room at a live event to consistently closing 40% or more. Then I started using it on my sales webinars and saw a dramatic increase in sales each time. It's worked so well and so consistently that I will never give a sales presentation again without it.

The big idea is that the only thing prospects remember when you sell is the last thing you showed them. He explained that most sales presentations focus on the core offer, then a list of bonuses and a call to action. So all people remember is the last bonus mentioned. If they don't think the last thing you offered is worth the price, they simply won't buy.

Remember the stack slide you made back in Secret #9? It's time to use it. As you go through the offer with your audience, you'll explain the first element of your offer, then show it on the stack slide, all by itself. Then reveal the second element of your offer, and come back to the stack slide that shows the first element along with the second one. You do this for each element in the offer—you talk about it, then add it to the stack slide. So the audience sees the value adding up. The LAST thing you show them before you reveal the price is the full stack slide with the entire offer. When you present this way, the audience associates the price with the FULL OFFER, and not just the last thing you mentioned.

I'm going to walk you through all the slides I normally use with my stack, so you can see how this works. I always lead in with the transition question from the last chapter, then I start revealing what they're going to get.

27. What You're Gonna Get...

Here I usually show a digital image representing the course content. I explain that when they invest right away, they will get instant access to my masterclass.

28. Quick High-Level Recap of Deliverables

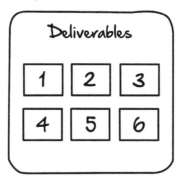

A big mistake people make is going deep into each module explaining what will be covered each week. Don't do that. It overwhelms and confuses your audience. Just give them a high-level look at each module. Go through this really quickly. It should only take about 30 seconds.

Here's what we're going to cover. Week 1, we're going to talk about _____. Week 2, we'll go over _____. Week 3, we dive into _____. Then by Week 4, you'll be ready for _____. Week 5 we look at _____. And finally, in Week 6, we wrap it all up with _____.

Now let me show you some people who've had a chance to go through this...

29. Show 3 Case Studies

Here you will highlight the success stories from the beta group you ran earlier. Over time, you'll add in other success stories as they happen.

Let me introduce you to... (*Tell Case Study #1.*)
Then there's... (*Tell Case Study #2.*)
And probably my favorite story is... (*Tell Case Study #3.*)

30. Who This Works For (All-Inclusive)

After you present the case studies, people often think: *That's great, but it won't work for me.* They think: *That person lives in Australia.* Or *That*

person is in a different industry. They think their business or personal circumstances are different from the case study details, so it won't work for them. This is where you make a blanket statement about all the different people it works for. Be as inclusive as possible here.

> So I want to go back and make sure you realize who this is for.
>
> (*Business example*) It's for people just starting out or those who are already successful and want to scale.
>
> (*Weight loss example*) It's for people who have 100 pounds to lose or those who only have five more to go. It even helps people who don't need to lose weight, but want to build healthy muscle.

31. Destroy the #1 Reason People Don't Get Started

Usually there's a common reason people don't get started right away. It's the elephant in the room. Address it head on so they don't keep thinking about it through the rest of your presentation. The biggest excuse I hear with ClickFunnels is that they don't have a product to sell yet. So I tell them they don't need to have a product. They can use affiliate products. And we actually teach them how to make a product, if that's what they want to do. Destroy your audience's #1 objection about the training right here.

You might be thinking you can't get started with this because... Here's why that's a mistake that will hold you back from success...

32. Stack Slide #1

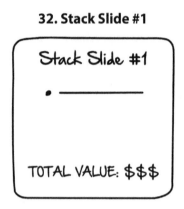

Reveal the first stack slide with the six-week masterclass on it. Be sure to include the value of the item on the slide.

When you sign up, you're going to get instant access to my six-week masterclass, a total value of $_____.

33. Introduce Element #2: The Tools

It's time to introduce the tools you created on your stack slide in Secret #11. I tell them that when they invest today, they will also receive this extra cool thing. Quickly review the tools they're going to get. Don't go too deep or you'll overwhelm people.

> As part of this package, you're going to get… It's a tool to help you …

34. You'll Be Able To… / You'll Be Able to Get Rid Of…

I want them to realize that investing in this thing shouldn't cost them any money, it should only save them money. So remind them what they are now able to do, but also what they will be able to get rid of. Hopefully the money they save will be more than what they are actually paying. That way, it's a truly irresistible offer.

> When you have this tool, you'll be able to _____.
> When you have this tool, you'll be able to get rid of _____.

35. The Problem This Tool Solved for You

When I was first figuring this stuff out, I ran into a big roadblock. I didn't know how to _____. So I had to create _____ for myself.

36. How Much Time / Money This Tool Will Save Them

Talk about all the time and money you had to spend to overcome that big roadblock that the tool saved you from. Maybe you had to spend a year developing email templates, or you had to hire expensive lawyers to draft just the right contracts. Then explain that they won't have to because you're just going include the tool for them.

Way back then, I had to spend _____ and _____
to figure out an efficient way to handle this problem. But I don't
want you to have to recreate the wheel. I've already got proven
_____. And I'm just going to give it / them to you with
this package. Sound cool?

When you use this tool, not only do you save the time and money
I spent to develop it, but you also save what could be months or years
of wasted time and money because you'll be doing it right the first time.
There's no trial and error period.

37. Break Related Beliefs About the Tools

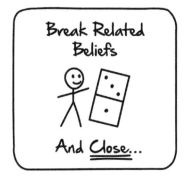

As we've done in other sections, here I mention any false beliefs they
may have about the tools or their abilities to use them, and I quickly
break and rebuild those belief patterns.

38. Stack Slide #2

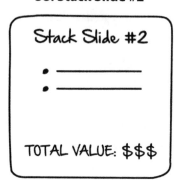

This is where the magic starts happening. Show the stack slide again with the masterclass on top and the tools on the second line. Then update the total value price at the bottom to show what the offer is now worth.

39. Introduce Tangible By-Product #1 (Related to Secret #1)

Here you introduce the next component of the offer they'll receive when they invest. It's the tangible by-product you identified previously.

When you invest today, you're also going to get access to _____, which will help you with _____.

40. Pain and Cost

Here you talk again about the pain and cost you had to go through to create this first by-product.

> I had to go through _____ and _____ to get _____. But you won't have to because I'm giving you _____ as a special bonus.

41. Ease and Speed for Them

Whatever the pain and cost was to you doesn't matter, because the bonus is going to make it easier and faster for them to get results.

This bonus is going to make it faster and easier for you to
_____. How? Because it _____.

42. Break Related Beliefs

As we've done in other sections, here I discuss any false beliefs they may have about the bonus or their abilities to use it. Then I quickly break and rebuild those belief patterns.

43. Stack Slide #3

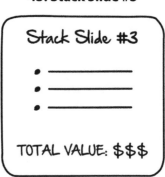

Do you see how this works now? You mention an element, then add it to the stack. Mention another element and add it to the stack. Sometimes you may feel you're getting repetitive, but that is the key. It helps your audience understand the offer completely. The first few times I did this, I felt silly each time I re-stacked it. But after I added it, and started closing 300% more people during my presentations, I quickly stopped feeling silly. This is the KEY to success when selling to the masses.

44.–53. Introduce Your Other Two Tangible By-Products

Repeat steps 39 through 43 for your second and third tangibles. Show the pain and costs you had to go through to create it, then show the ease and speed of use this will create for them. Break any false beliefs, then stack again.

After you've done that for the second and third tangibles, you have your full stack slide.

54. Stack Slide #5 (The Big Stack)

I call this the Big Stack slide, because it has the entire contents of your offer, including the value of each piece. You also want to total everything up and have the value be 10 times as much as the actual price will be. (If the value doesn't reach that level, consider adding something more valuable to your offer.) It should look something like this.

What You're Gonna Get...

- **6 Weeks Funnel Hacks Masterclass** ($2,997 Value)
- **ClickFunnels: 6 Month Enterprise Account** ($3,564 Value)
- **Instant Traffic Hacks** ($1,997 Value)
- **Inception Secrets** ($1,997 Value)
- **Soap / Seinfeld Secrets** ($997 Value)
- **Unlimited Funnels In Your Account (First 50 Only)** (Priceless!)

Total Value: $11,552

click funnels   #funnelhacker

55. If / All Statements

If / All

① Vehicle
② Internal
③ External

Now that we've given them the big value price, we need to convince them that this offer is actually worth that much and get them to admit it to themselves. We do that by using something Dave Vanhoose calls "If / All" statements.

An If / All statement reads like this: "If all this package did was _____ would it be worth $_____?"

I usually transition by saying something like: "Now obviously, I'm not going to charge you $11,552. But If I DID charge you $11,552, and all it did was _____, would it be worth it to you?"

Then do three If / All statements based on your three secrets.

Vehicle (Secret #1)

If all this system did / got you was _____ (related to Secret #1), would it be worth $_____?

STOP and wait for them to indicate yes.

Internal (Secret #2)

And if all it did was _____ (related to Secret #2), would it be worth $_____?

STOP and wait for them to indicate yes.

External (Secret #3)

And what if all it did was _____ (related to Secret #3), then would it be worth it?

STOP and wait for them to indicate yes.

They've now said yes 3 times when you asked them if what you are selling is actually worth the total value, usually a 10-time markup. Now when you discount the price to what you're actually selling it for, they are getting a 90% discount from what they believe (and have said) it's worth.

56. I Had 2 Choices

I like to use the "I had two choices" close at this point because it gets them to agree that you should charge them more in order to make the program better.

> I had two choices with this. I could go as cheap as possible and try to sell as many as possible. But the problem with that is I couldn't really stack on the value for you. So I decided to go with a second option, which obviously requires a slightly higher investment on your side. But in exchange for that, we can dedicate more time, energy, and resources to help guarantee your success.

57. What Would the End Result be Worth?

Before you reveal the actual price, ask them what the end result would be worth to them.

So if you had a successful funnel today that was making you money, what would it be worth to you?

And then I STOP and wait for them to answer that question in their minds.

How much would you pay to have that one successful funnel?

And then I STOP and wait for them to think about it for a few seconds.

You can probably see why people pay \$_____ for a similar result from me…because it's not a cost—it's an INVESTMENT.

58. Price Drop

Now I come back to the full price I showed them right before the If / All statements.

You've already seen how it's worth $_____.

And even at $_____, which I charge the public, it's a great deal.

But because of _____, I'm going to give you a very special offer...

59. Price Reveal

Here is the first time you reveal the actual price. Tell them the real price and give your first call to action (asking them to click on a button, go to a certain website, or call a phone number). Every slide after this will have a call to action link, so when they are ready, they can sign up.

60. Price Justification

For years, I ended my sales presentations with the price on the last slide. As I gained experience, I realized that the elements that come AFTER the initial price reveal are vitally important to closing the sale. So we give the initial price, and some people will still have sticker shock. I need to let that price marinate for a while as I justify why it's actually not that expensive.

My first price justification is usually related to either showing them what the full price would be outside of the current presentation or comparing it to the price of other options for getting a similar result (apples vs. oranges).

> (*Full price example*) Now let me put this into perspective for you. If you went to my regular website right now, you could buy this same product for $_____. But because you've invested this time with me, and you've proven that you really want to get this result, I'm making a special offer just for this webinar.
>
> (*Apples vs. oranges example*) If you were to hire a professional to do this for you, it might cost $_____. But because you're learning how to do it yourself AND I'm giving you all the tools and resources to make it happen fast, you only pay $_____.

61. You've Got 2 Choices

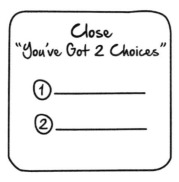

Now I like to mention the choices they can make.

So at this point you have two choices. Choice #1 is to do nothing. If you do nothing with the information you've learned over the last hour, what will you get? Nothing.

Or you can choose to take a leap of faith. Just test it out to see if it will work for you.

62. Guarantee

Then I reveal that it's okay if it doesn't work for them, because they're covered with our 30-day money-back guarantee. They can test-drive it now and see if it will work for them. They have nothing to lose.

63. The Real Question is This...

Now that they know they have nothing to lose, I like to make their choice as simple as possible. Help them see that this really is a no-brainer.

The real question is this: Is it worth gambling a few minutes of your time to check this out? Even if it only does HALF of what I've claimed today, it will pay for itself as soon as _____.

64. Stack Slide

Next I show them the Big Stack slide one last time, with everything they're going to get and the total value. I go through each element line by line one last time to cement the offer in their minds before my final pitch.

65. Urgency / Scarcity Bonus

The two most valuable tools in marketing are urgency and scarcity. Here you're going to add a bonus upgrade that's only available right then. You can create urgency and scarcity by offering something special to a certain number of people, or for a certain amount of time (or both).

Do not skip this part! It is the key to getting people to buy immediately. If they leave the webinar, the chances of them coming back and buying later are almost zero. In fact, I usually give a bonus only for those who are actually on live that I don't offer to those who only watch the replays later. That encourages people to show up live, but it also gives them a reason to sign up before the presentation is over. The deadline is the key.

66. Closing Call to Action / Q&A Slide

This is the slide I end my presentation with, and it stays up during the entire question and answer session. There are a few key components to this slide.

- Recap of the offer
- Countdown clock for 30 minutes
- Price
- Call to action

Then it's time to answer questions.

Sometimes I'll take questions live from the audience, and other times I'll actually pre-write many of the questions I know people typically have. I then go through those questions, and give another call to action after each one. That gives me lots of opportunities to repeat the link for people to buy.

I also try to think about any other false beliefs they may still have, then use our sentence: "You're probably thinking _____, right?"

And that is the stack. That single concept has made me more money than anything else I've ever done in this business. Study it. Master it. There is no greater gift I could give you than this.

TRIAL CLOSES

CLOSES STACK

LET ME ASK YOU A QUESTION

Money Is Good	Disposable Income	Money Replenishes	Break Old Habits
Information Alone?	Money or Excuses?	Your 2 Choices	Their 2 Choices
Us VS Them	The Hand Hold	Say Goodbye	Now & Later
Only Excuses	Reluctant Hero	If You Only Got	Close Close

use two types of closes in my presentations. The first type, "trial closes", I use almost every 60 seconds or less. The other I use throughout the stack. You'll want to use both kinds in your presentations as well. Let's take a look at each of them and how they work.

TRIAL CLOSES

Years ago, I had heard rumors of a guy nicknamed "The Pied Piper of Real Estate". His real name is Ted Thomas, and he is a real estate speaker famous for being so good at selling from the stage that he would have hundreds of people line up behind him, waving their credit cards in the air and walk with him to the back of the room to buy his program. One day I had the chance to witness this in person, and it was one of the coolest things I had ever seen.

A few years later, I was speaking at an event and noticed that Ted was in the audience. I was so nervous. One of the best closers in the world was about to watch me try to close this room. I did my best to ignore the butterflies in my stomach and delivered a pretty good presentation. While I did get a lot of signups, I didn't get a huge table rush.

After my presentation, Ted introduced himself and invited me to lunch. As we ate, he started asking me casual questions. After a few minutes, he started to grin. I asked him why he was smiling. He laughed and said, "What's your head doing right now?" I realized I was nodding my head up and down—and had been since the moment we started talking.

He said, "What I've been doing is a little technique I call trial closes." I've been asking you dozens of little yes-or-no questions where the only answer is yes. You instantly started nodding, and you didn't stop until I pointed it out just now."

He then went on to explain that the reason I didn't get a table rush was because the first time I asked the audience to say yes was when I was asking for their money. "When you watch me speak, you'll notice that all the heads in the audience are nodding the entire time. I am constantly asking simple questions to get people to say yes over and over again, so when I ask them to give me money at the end, they've already told me yes hundreds of times before that."

I thought that was pretty cool. But to be completely honest, I thought he was over-simplifying his skills. I didn't think his trial closes could possibly have that big of an impact on sales. But I decided to test it out.

At the time, I had an automated webinar that had been running profitably for five or six months. I listened to the recording and found a few dozen places where I could add in trial closes. I recorded just the trial closes and inserted them into the audio file. I didn't expect much, but what happened was amazing! That webinar went from making $9.45 per registrant to $16.50 per registrant—just by me adding in the trial closes.

From that day forward, I was sold. I wrote out simple trial closes on note cards and put them around my desk. As I worked through my various presentations, every time I'd see a card, I'd use that trial close. Here are some examples of trial closes that I've used dozens of times in each of my presentations.

- Are you ready to get started?
- Are you all getting this?
- Is this making sense?
- Can you imagine if that happened to you?
- Who here wants a free copy of _____?
- Would you like to be our next case study?
- You've heard them talk about this before, right?
- Isn't that cool?
- Isn't that exciting?
- Am I right?
- Can you see yourself doing _____?
- I'm sure you've noticed this too, right?

I could go on and on. It's become ingrained in how I write and speak. You've seen me using trial closes throughout this book, haven't you? (See what I did there?) (Whoa! I did it again, didn't I?) Get used to using lots of little statements that get your audience to think or say yes over and over again. The more you can get them to say yes, the more likely they will accept the epiphanies you've shared with them and the offer presented. Trial closes are a huge part of telling effective stories.

THE 16 CLOSES

When you get to the end of the presentation and start the stack, there are lots of really good closes you can use. But I have 16 favorites that I use repeatedly. Several listed here I've learned from Jason Fladlien's Webinar Pitch Secrets 2.0 (pages 34-43), who has kindly let me share them for you in this book. I don't use all of them in all presentations, but I pick a handful of those that help strengthen my argument.

I already built some of my favorites into the stack for you above. I want to show you all of them though, so you can pick and choose which ones to plug in to your presentations. Some will work better than others for different types of presentations. So just choose the ones that flow naturally and make the most sense.

For each close below, I will briefly explain the concept then show you how I would use that close in my own presentations.

Money is Good: The goal is to get people to disassociate their fear about spending money with you. Money is a tool for exchange. You spend money to get something greater in return.

> So I want you to think about something for a minute. What is money? A lot of people have fear about money, and even bigger fears about spending money, but you need to understand that money is good. It's just a tool that was created for exchange.
>
> Other than that, there is no real value in money. You can't use it to stay warm, you can't eat it, you can only trade it for something else that you want. Just think, everyone who exchanges money for something does it because they feel that what they are getting in exchange is greater than keeping the money or using it for something else. At least that's what I expect when I buy something. I don't actually know for sure until I do buy it and try it out, and can see the results.

But my question for you is this. Would you exchange that money for those results? If the answer is yes, then you need to get started right now. And if you have any fear that it might not be what you expected, or that you might not be able to get those results, just let us know, and we'll give you your money back.

Disposable Income: The goal is to help them realize that they are spending the disposable income on things that aren't serving them well, and by spending that money on things that will help them grow, they will have long-term fulfillment. When you use the Disposable Income close, they get that they DO have the money to invest.'

> Most people in this world live paycheck to paycheck. Every couple of weeks you get paid and then you pay your fixed costs like rent and food. Then there's usually some money left over. We call that disposable income.
>
> Most people are going to blow that every single month. If they have $1,000 in disposable income, they're going to spend it until it's gone. They might spend it on movies or ice cream or travel—all short-term pleasures that are gone in an instant.
>
> But the cool thing is that money replenishes. Every two weeks—boom! There's another $1,000 in disposable income you can spend. Most people spend that cash on things that don't really add value to their lives in a meaningful way. You should be investing that money into products, programs, and services that will actually help you.
>
> That's the power of disposable income—it comes back. Every two weeks—boom! There's more money

Money Replenishes: The goal for this close is to help people realize that while each month money comes back, time does not, and if they're not careful, they will run out of time.

> Do you think it's okay to dip into your savings or leverage your credit and spend money you might not have to get started today? This is a serious question. Do you think it's okay or not? Some people say yes and some say no. Let's talk about this for a minute.
>
> Every month, money replenishes, right? But this is the key—time does NOT replenish. It disappears. So you could go out and spend months or years of your valuable time to figure something out—but you will never get that time back. Instead, you could save that time and effort, because I've already spent it for you, and work directly with me instead. It will cost you money to get started, but that money will come back, whereas the time away from your family in trial and error is wasted effort and is gone forever.

Break Old Habits: The goal for this close is to help them realize that if they leave today without investing, nothing in their life will change.

> Habits are really hard to change. I could leave the webinar right now and go enjoy the rest of the afternoon. I'm already successful with _____. This is already working for me. But this is not about me. This is about you. If YOU leave now, you might think you learned a lot of cool stuff, but my guess is that by morning tomorrow you'll have already slipped back into your normal routines. Right? You'd just do what you've always done. That's what most people do.

But because I'm your coach, your friend, your mentor, I'm not going to let you go back to your old habits. I'm going to make sure you're successful by breaking them. If you want real, lasting change, you need repeated exposure to the full system. That's what you'll get when you invest today.

Information Alone: My goal for this close is to help them understand that, while they have gotten some awesome information, they can't rely on information alone. They need coaching and accountability, too.

So now I've told you how the whole system works. I've shown you how you can _____. I've shown you that you only need _____ to make this all work. But you know what? To be successful with this, you're going to need more than information alone.

I know you can be successful with this system, but you're going to need coaching. You will have questions that need answering. And you might need help in the accountability department, too. Let me tell you, I take my job as a coach very seriously. I won't let you quit on yourself. We will get through everything together. I can't do that with just a few videos and some PDFs. Information alone won't cut it.

My success rate when people go at this by themselves is almost 0%. But my success rate for those who work with me is closer to _____%. If information were enough, then you could have just turned to Google. You need a guide who has been there before, who can take you there right now.

Money or Excuses: The goal of this close is to get them to quit making excuses about why they can't buy.

I've been in this business a long time. And I've found there are only two kinds of people. Those who are good at (making money, losing weight, etc.) and those who are good at making excuses. You can't be both. If you're the one making excuses…I hate to say it, but I think you're going to have a really hard time _____.

The good news is that you get to choose. In this moment, you can choose which type of person you're going to be. Don't be someone who makes excuses, be someone who actually _____.

Your Two Choices: The goal of this close is for them to understand why you are charging so much money, and to make sure they are okay with that.

When we were deciding how to price this, we had two choices. The first was to go as cheap as possible and sell as many as we could. Now the problem with that is we would have no real incentive to pile on the value. It would cost us more for those bonuses than the whole course would be worth. Our second choice was to raise the price a little, and give you absolutely everything you need to succeed.

Their Two Choices: The goal for this close is to help them realize they are crazy if they don't invest with you today.

The way I see it, you've got two choices. Your first option is to do nothing and not take this leap of faith (which is 100% risk free).

Your second option is to pony up this tiny investment today (compared to all the value you'll get in return) and just give it a shot. See if it'll work for you. If it doesn't—for whatever reason—you get your money back. There's no risk. You have nothing to lose but the stress and headaches.

Us vs. Them The goal for this close is to call out people as either do-ers or dabblers.

I'm guessing there are two kinds of people listening to me right now. You're either a do-er or a dabbler. The dabblers love to sit and listen and learn, but they rarely ever do anything and often look for any excuse not to move forward.

Some of you are do-ers. You're not sure how this is going to work for you, but you see how it's worked for me and for other people, so you have faith that it will work for you as well. And what I've found is that it's the do-ers who get ahead in life, while the dabblers don't ever really seem to progress.

The Hand Hold: This close is where you actually walk them through the sign-up process.

When you are ready to change your life, this is what you need to start doing. First, open up a browser window—I don't care if it's Google Chrome, Firefox, Safari. I'm going to open Chrome right now and show you how this works.

Type in www._____.com. On this page, you're going to see _____. Then you're going to click here and fill out this form. After that, you'll be taken to this page, where you can create your account. If you have any issues, this link will connect you to my support desk, where _____ can answer any of your questions.

Say Goodbye: In this close I want to show them all the pain that will instantly disappear after they invest.

> Once you've been through this training and have everything set up, you can say goodbye to the stress of _____. You'll never have to worry about _____ again. Can you imagine what life will be like when those things have instantly disappeared from your life? What will you do with all the extra (time, energy, money, etc.)?

Now & Later: In this close, I want to paint a picture of their life now compared to what it could become if they invest.

> So I want to paint a picture of where I was before I started with (the new opportunity). I struggled with _____. I wasn't able to _____. Things were hard because _____. Does that sound familiar?
>
> But now I want you to get a vision of what life could be like. Ever since (new opportunity), I've been able to _____. Now I'm able to _____, and things are amazing. Can you imagine what that would be like?

Only Excuses: The goal of this close is to call out any excuses that might be keeping them back, and then diffuse them.

> If you didn't sign up immediately, you're probably thinking one of two things. First, you might be thinking _____. Don't worry. We spend the whole first module showing you _____. I'm also going to show you how we figured out _____. I'm going to give you templates to help you figure

it out. I promise you, by the end of Week 1, you'll know exactly how to _____.

Second, you're probably a little nervous about setting it all up. I get that. But I promise you, it's not hard. On Week 2, we're going to walk step-by-step through the whole setup process. I know _____ can be scary, but we'll be there for you.

The third reason might be that you think it's too expensive. If that's your reason, I don't know how I can help you. This is an investment and a decision you need to make for yourself. When I invested in learning this process, I paid $_____, but I got back _____ within _____.

Reluctant Hero: The goal of this close is to help them believe they can actually do it.

I want you to know something about me. I'm no one special. I don't have any supernatural gifts or anything. I actually really struggle with _____. And that's what I love about this system—I don't have to worry about that anymore!

If You Only Got: The goal of this close is to show them what they already got for free, and what they can possibly achieve when they invest with you.

Okay, so I could stop right here. If I stopped right here and you only got _____, it would still be worth the investment, right? But you're also getting _____ and _____. But you're also going to get _____ and _____ and _____. I want to make sure that nothing is standing in the way of your success.

Close Close: This close is the final push to get them over the edge. I typically do this one several times during the question and answer section at the end of the webinar.

> If you're still on the fence, now is the time to open a new browser window, go to www._____.com, and get started. Remember there is no risk, and we have a 100% money-back guarantee. But the only way for you to know if this is right for you is to get started right now. You can get your account at _____.com.

There you go—16 closes you can use throughout the stack to help sell your offer. I like to use a close right before I introduce a new element in the stack. Sometimes I'll even use two or three closes in between elements. They just flow naturally one into the other.

At this point, you know how to deliver a Perfect Presentation. Now it's time to look at the different funnels you'll use and how you'll work this system week after week.

SECTION FOUR

THE FUNNELS

As we move into Section Four, let's look at how far you've come. You've started your own mass movement by identifying your attractive character, creating your future-based cause, and creating your new opportunity. You've learned how to create belief by telling stories the right way. You've built out a sales presentation that tells your stories in a way that will create intense desire for people to buy in to your new opportunity. And you've learned to create a stack that will cause them to take action.

The next step is getting the right people to come into a selling environment where you can deliver your message and encourage people to follow you into your new opportunity. You do that by creating sales funnels using a software tool called ClickFunnels and then filling those funnels with qualified prospects. That's what this next section is all about. It's the fuel for your fire. When you master this piece, you'll have a constant stream of people to share your message with.

THE PERFECT WEBINAR MODEL

For those who have been in this information business for a while, this next section will be counterintuitive. You will fight me on it, because in the past you've made money by creating an offer, selling it to your audience, then creating another product the next month to sell to those same people. When I tell you that you need to do the EXACT same webinar every week for the next 12 months (minimum), you're going to think I'm crazy. Yet this model took my company from $0 to $10 million within 12 months, and then to $30 million just 12 months later.

For the first 10 years of my business, I focused on building a cult-ure of people who loved what I did. Then I stopped bringing in new people. I had my following and I would sell them something new each month. A percentage of the people would buy and the rest would say no. The only way I could make more money the following month was to create a new product and sell it to this same list of people. So we'd create a new product, launch it, get paid, then start all over again for the next month. This is how most experts run their businesses these days.

For me, this was a horrible cycle, which forced me to create new things every month. I had no leverage, and my company always maxed out at about $1–3 million a year.

Then one day I had a chance to talk to one of my friends MaryEllen Tribby. MaryEllen has a unique ability to take companies that are doing well and quickly scale them to much higher profitability. One of her successes was with a company called Weiss Research. She took them from $11 million in sales to $67 million in just 12 months. She had similar results with several other companies. I asked her to share her secret. How could she possibly grow a company that fast?

She said, "Internet marketers like you are so smart and so dumb at the same time."

I was a little shocked, but she had my interest. "What do you mean?"

She went on to say that what we do each month is the equivalent of creating a Broadway show. "You hire the best screenwriters in the world. You hire the best actors. You practice for months, then you open the show in downtown Boise, Idaho. (Because that's where you happen to live and you spend a month promoting it.) You open the show to a sold-out crowd and they give you a standing ovation. That night after the show is done, you pull everything down and start writing your next play to open next month in the same auditorium in Boise."

I kinda laughed nervously, then asked, "Okay, then what should I be doing? What would you do differently?"

"I take companies like yours that have an awesome show in Boise—I take them on the road. I take that show to Chicago, to New York, to LA, and I keep running it until it stops making money."

I realized then and there what I was doing wrong. I needed to learn how to take my show on the road. In other words, learn how to drive more traffic to the same webinar every week. After I understood that principle, I sketched out a model, and told my team I was going to stick to this model for the next 12 months. This is what it looked like.

THE MODEL

This model is based on a live event schedule. My favorite day to do webinars is Thursday, because then I have adequate time to promote it during the week.

I start my promotions on Monday and keep pushing hard until Thursday before the webinar. I send emails. I drive Facebook ads. I work with joint venture partners, and a whole bunch of other activities that drive traffic to my sign-up page. Whatever I can do to get people onto this live event, I do. When the webinar starts, I stop all promotion because the rest of the week is about converting those prospects into buyers.

Every market is different, but I like to spend only $3–$5 per webinar registrant. If the costs are getting above that, then my landing page isn't right, my message isn't interesting, I'm targeting the wrong people, or something else is off. As your costs climb higher into the $7–$8 range, it becomes challenging to stay profitable on the front end. Here are my personal goals for this funnel each week. Your goals may be different, but this will give you an idea what to shoot for.

$3 Per Registrant ➜ 1,000 Registrants Per Week ($3k Ad Spend)
➜ 25% Show-up Rate (250 People)
➜ 10% Close Rate @ $997 (25 Sales / $25k)
➜ Double Sales on Follow-Up Replays (Additional $25k)

With that formula, I'm putting $3,000 a week into ads and making back $50,000 a week in sales, while adding 1,000 new people to my list! Those are the goals each week. Some weeks, we don't get the full 1,000 registered; other times we'll get 2,500 people or more. But setting that as the goal and doing a webinar every week (yes, the SAME webinar over and over again) is the recipe for new consistent leads and cash flow into your company.

So each week I do a LIVE webinar selling people on my new opportunity. I spend Monday through Thursday morning promoting that webinar to get as many people as possible to show up on Thursday night. I present the webinar live on Thursday night and make my special offer. Then I show replays on Friday, Saturday, and Sunday. At midnight Sunday, I take down the offer for those who had registered. Then I start again on Monday filling my event for the upcoming Thursday. That's it. That's the whole model.

The next question I get from people when I explain this to them live is, "But Russell, inside of ClickFunnels, I can create an automated webinar. Can't I just automate this so I don't have to do it live every week?" And my answer is yes…eventually—but right now, you HAVE to do it live.

I recommend presenting the webinar live a few dozen times (at least) before you ever automate it, and here's why: My Funnel Hacks presentation has made me over $10 million dollars within the first year.

The first time I delivered it, I did it at a live seminar and was able to close 33% of the people in the room. Not too shabby, right?

The next day, as I was leaving the event, one of the attendees who heard the presentation told me she loved it, but since she was a coach and didn't have a supplement to sell, she couldn't use ClickFunnels.

I gave her a puzzled look.

She pointed out that all the examples I had showed were people selling supplements, but she didn't have one. I told her that I use ClickFunnels for my coaching business, and showed her a few of my funnels. She got so excited, she ran back into the event and grabbed two of her friends. They all filled out order forms and handed them to me before I left the hotel. I closed three people who hadn't signed up before!

This interaction showed that my presentation wasn't perfect. So on my flight home, I tweaked it by adding a few more slides showing different funnels and giving examples of how other industries can use ClickFunnels.

The next week, I did the presentation live to about 600 entrepreneurs on a webinar. When it was over, we had sold about $30k, which wasn't too bad. But I knew it should have been more. I had to deliver the webinar again in a few hours to another group of entrepreneurs, so I tweaked it again. I exported all the questions people had asked, reviewed them, then changed my slides based on the questions they had during my presentation. I saw all the spots where I had explained things wrong or didn't give enough detail or flat-out missed things people actually wanted.

Four hours later, I delivered this revised presentation to about 500 entrepreneurs, and this time we sold $120k live! I repeated this same process 60+ times over the next 12 months—doing a live webinar, exporting questions, and adjusting the presentation.

It's probably why one of my friends and conversion experts, Joe Lavery, said this after watching my presentation:

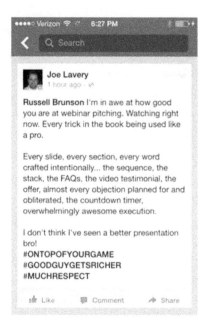

So yes, eventually I will suggest that you automate the webinar, but not at first. You need to get people's feedback, make changes, and perfect your webinar. It's more work, but the result could be worth tens of millions of dollars to you over time.

Now I'm sure some of you saw that I'm spending over $3,000 per week on Facebook alone to get people into my webinar, and got a little nervous. Don't worry about that now. In Secret #22, I will be showing you ways to fill your funnel with the right people who are ready to buy. There are methods (like the Facebook strategy) that cost money, but there are other ways that you can get people to attend your webinars for free. When you are spending money, start with a lower ad budget at first. Run your webinar a few times to get the kinks out and know what conversion rates to expect. Then you can spend more money on ads because you'll know what kind of return to expect.

In the beginning, all kinds of things could happen. Facebook could mess up your ads. Your webinar software could fail to record or function right. You could lose power in the middle of your broadcast. Things happen. Sometimes no one even shows up at all!

It's important not to get discouraged. Stick to the plan, and work it week in and week out. The beginning can be rough for some people. Don't quit! It won't be long before you start hitting consistent numbers. Now that you know the model, let's take a look at the funnel you'll be using to move people from registration through the purchase.

PERFECT WEBINAR FUNNEL

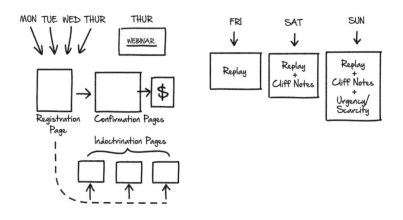

STEP 1: SEND TRAFFIC TO THE WEBINAR REGISTRATION PAGE.

Coming up in Secret #22 (Fill Your Funnel), I'll show you how to get people into your funnel, but for now let's look at the actual funnel itself, starting with the registration page. I wanted to share a few things you should do on your registration page to get the most people to register.

The key to a high-converting webinar registration page is... CURIOSITY.

That's it. If your registration page isn't converting well, it's because you're showing people too much and they assume they know the answer. If they think they know what you're going to talk about, then they won't register or show up. If they can't figure out what it is without registering, then you'll get them to register AND show up.

The headline I showed you earlier, "How to _____ without _____", is typically the key to getting people to register. Here is an example of the type of headline I used on my Funnel Scripts webinar:

Sometimes I tweak my headline to increase the curiosity factor. This is the main registration page we used the first year for the Funnel Hacks webinar.

I want you to notice a few things about this page.

1. **The picture makes NO sense.** When you look at it, you have no idea what it is or why I'm doing it. It arouses curiosity. Find a picture of you that's kinda related to the topic but kinda strange to help increase your conversions dramatically. I do NOT recommend putting video on a webinar registration page. Rarely (if ever) will it beat a strange image. But if you do a video, be sure to test the page without a video as well.

2. **The headline builds a TON of curiosity.**
   My Weird Niche Funnel That's Currently Making Me $17,947 Per Day...And How You Can ETHICALLY Knock It Off In Less Than 10 Minutes!

   This headline gives you a hint about the presentation, but it leaves SO many unanswered questions.
   • What niche is it?
   • Is it really possible to make $17,947 per day?
   • Can you really ETHICALLY knock it off? How?
   • In just 10 minutes?

3. **The page uses urgency and scarcity.** Nothing gets people to act (register, show up, and buy) better than urgency and scarcity. These are your secret weapons—use them.

STEP 2: SEND REGISTRANTS TO A THANK-YOU PAGE WITH A SELF-LIQUIDATING OFFER.

After people register, we take them to a thank-you page where we give them the basic information for the webinar. On this page, I DO like to include a video, with me talking about why I'm so excited for the webinar. They NEED to feel my passion for the subject or they won't show up. Remember, the registration page is about curiosity. The thank-you page is about your passion and excitement for what they are about to experience on the webinar.

One of the biggest secrets about the thank-you page is that you can (and should) use it to sell people something! We call this a "self-liquidating offer" or SLO. There are a few reasons you want to include this offer here.

1. Self-liquidating offer means it liquidates your ad costs. That's right—often you can completely cover your ad costs from the product you offer on your thank-you page. That means everything you sell on the webinar is pure profit!
2. If they buy something that complements what the webinar is about, they are more likely to show up live.
3. Buyers in motion tend to stay in motion, unless you do something to offend them. That means if they buy from you BEFORE the webinar, they are a lot more likely to buy from you ON the webinar.

I like my SLO offers to be lower ticket, usually $37–$47 or a free (or $1) trial to a membership site. When we launched the Funnel Hacks webinar, we decided to give away a free trial to ClickFunnels on the thank-you page. (Honestly, it was more of an afterthought, but we did it anyway.) Looking at the stats from the first year of following this model, more than 15,000 people have created ClickFunnels trials from that link, and over 4,500 are still active. If you do the math, we have over $450k a MONTH in recurring cash coming in just from our thank-you page!

STEP 3: SEND A SERIES OF INDOCTRINATION EMAILS.
Between the time someone registers for the webinar to the time you deliver it live, there are about 10 million distractions that could keep them from showing up. If you're not careful, the people you paid for with advertising won't remember who you are by Thursday.

So during the in-between time, I send registrants videos to help introduce them to my philosophy, get them excited about the webinar, and presell them. For me, each of the videos is pre-selling them on one of my 3 Secrets. Remember, each of the 3 Secrets is tied to a false belief pattern. So I make a video talking about that belief pattern, and then tell them that the webinar will help them discover why that isn't true, and why the opposite IS actually true. Don't answer the questions, just increase the curiosity for what they're going to learn on the webinar.

The main concern people share with this sequence is "But what if they register on Wednesday and they only get one or two of the indoctrination emails before the webinar?"

Here's the thing—the indoctrination sequence is NOT essential to the sale. It's an amplifier. If they only see one video and then they attend the webinar, that's okay. Videos 2 and 3 may come after the webinar, and that's fine. Don't stress about it. Oftentimes one of the indoctrination emails is the thing that gets them to watch a replay or to purchase after the webinar is over.

STEP 4: SEND REMINDERS.

The reminders start on Wednesday. Just send quick emails and / or text messages that say something like: "Hey, don't forget we're talking about _____ LIVE tomorrow at _____." People don't always read every email, so I like to send one the day before we go live, one the morning of the webinar, one an hour or so before we start, another about 15 minutes before, then a final one that says, "We're live—join us!"

STEP 5: PRESENT THE WEBINAR LIVE.

I like to present my webinars on Thursdays. Others might prefer Tuesdays or Wednesdays, but that matters less than following the pre-webinar indoctrination series, the Perfect Webinar script, and the follow-up sequences. For the actual webinar, here are a few things to keep in mind.

1. The webinar should be about 90 minutes long. The first 60 minutes, you focus on breaking and rebuilding their false belief patterns. This is typically the hardest part for people to get right.

They try to teach, they try to share cool stuff, and they don't understand why they don't get lots of sales. The core teaching is identifying their false belief patterns. If you do this right, the product will sell easily. If you do it wrong, you'll struggle. Review the Perfect Webinar section a dozen times until you master the section on belief patterns.

2. The last 30 minutes is the pitch. You deliver that with the stack, and add in the closes. When the 90 minutes is over, I usually spend the remaining 15–30 minutes for Q & A, closing people between each question.

3. The best time of day for your webinar depends a lot on your market. I schedule my webinars during the day because most people in my market are entrepreneurs who usually have more freedom over their schedules during the day. Other markets where people have 9–5 jobs usually require nighttime webinars. So WHEN you present the webinar will depend on your particular audience.

4. I like presenting my live webinars on GoToWebinar.com. Some of my friends use WebinarJam or other software. Each system has pros and cons, so you have to figure out what's best for you.

5. Typically, about 25% of the registrants show up on the webinar. If fewer than 25% attend, focus more on the indoctrination sequence, sending text message reminders before the webinar, emails one hour before the webinar, and again 15 minutes before. You've paid a lot of money to get them registered, and you're going to have to push hard to get them to show up.

6. When I transition from the content to the pitch, I check how many people are still on the webinar, and I base my closing stats on that number. So if I have 250 people who are still on the webinar when I start the pitch at the 60-minute mark, and

I know that I typically close 15%, I'll probably make about $37,500.

What will your close rate be? At first, it will probably be pretty low. That's why you need to do it live so many times. When you have a 5% close rate, you have a good webinar and are likely going to be profitable on the front end. When you get it to 10%, then (I believe) you have a million-dollar-a-year webinar. When you get above 10%... Well, I'll just say that at 15%, we did just shy of $10 million the first year. So it pays to keep refining your conversion rates by tweaking and presenting live presentations.

STEP 6: SEND FOLLOW-UPS AND CREATE LAST-MINUTE URGENCY.

As soon as a webinar is over, we shift focus to the replay campaign. Some people get REALLY intense with their replay campaigns, but the basics are urgency and scarcity. That's what gets people to take action. I usually DOUBLE my sales between the time I end the webinar and when we close down the offer Sunday at midnight.

Friday, Saturday, and Sunday you will deliver follow-up emails including the webinar replay link. The first day, I talk about what a great response we had on the live call and offer them a chance to watch the replay...if they access it quickly. When the cart closes, the replay link disappears as well.

Sometimes in my follow-up sequence I'll send a PDF cheat sheet (similar to CliffsNotes) that briefly summarizes what we covered in the webinar or even a PDF version of my slides so they can see what we covered in the webinar. Some people are more visual learners who prefer to read text over watching a video. People are busy and they may not have time to go watch your 90-minute presentation—but they WILL scan over your PDF. In this email, I also remind them that the offer is only live until Sunday. These few days are all about amping up the urgency and scarcity. If people think they have all the time in the world to buy, they won't.

On the last day, I send a couple of emails reminding them that the cart closes at midnight. I recap the main reasons they should buy and leave it at that. It's amazing how many people will hit the Buy button one minute before midnight!

STEP 7: CLOSE THE CART.

Sunday at midnight, it's time to close the cart. The offer is done, and the Buy buttons are deactivated. That's it. You've completed your Perfect Webinar funnel.

REPEAT

Monday morning, you start all over again with Step 1: Driving Traffic. Each time you go through this process, you will improve. You'll figure out different ways of presenting that get more people to buy. You'll answer more questions. You'll fine-tune your ad targeting. The point is to never stop after one try—ESPECIALLY if you had disappointing results.

No one showed up for Liz Benny's first live webinar. She had a few hundred people registered, yet for some reason no one showed up. She had spent months preparing, and not a single soul attended. But she didn't give up. She kept refining her process. And she wound up making just over a million dollars in her first year.

Would that be okay with you? If you knew you could make six or seven figures in a year, would you keep going in the face of disappointment? Yeah…me, too.

What happens if you get great results from your first live webinar? Should you automate it and move on to something else? No! This is a huge mistake people make—automating too soon. I ran the Funnel

Hacking webinar 60+ times before we finally decided to automate it. One full year of the same webinar, week in and week out. Some weeks I did it 5 or 6 times. In fact, to this day I still do it live a few times a month.

By the time we finally automated it, that presentation was as tight as it could be. We had every objection covered. We knew exactly how to get traffic. We had just the right follow-up sequences. And now it's all down to the numbers. Because we spent so much time perfecting the webinar, we get predictable results from the automated version.

So the last step is to repeat your webinar. Again and again. Run it every week for a full year, and watch what happens to your bank account and your expert status.

THE 4-QUESTION CLOSE (FOR HIGH-TICKET OFFERS)

The webinar process and the Perfect Webinar script you've just learned works really well for offers between $297 and $2,997. But when you're selling more expensive offers, you need to add another step. Instead of just sending people to an order form, send them to a page where they fill out an application. Then get on the phone and interview them to see if they'd be a good fit for the program. This works for two reasons.

- **Reason #1:** It's much easier to sell a $2,997–$100,000 program on the phone. That extra step helps people feel more comfortable paying the higher dollar amounts.
- **Reason #2:** At the higher-level programs, you are typically going to be working more closely with people. You can screen them to make sure you'll enjoy working with them. If they aren't a good fit, then don't accept them into your programs.

In *DotComSecrets*, I shared a two-step phone script that works really well when you have sales people working for you. For that script to work, you need two people: a setter and a closer. It works amazingly well, but only when the expert ISN'T the one on the phone. At least in the beginning, you will be doing these sales calls yourself, and for that I recommend a completely different script.

THE 4-QUESTION CLOSE SCRIPT

I learned various parts of this strategy from a few different people. Dan Sullivan wrote a book called *The Question*, which this whole script is based on. Perry Belcher coached a few of my friends through the script, and Greg Cassar coached me and my Inner Circle through the process. Even though this is called the 4-Question Close Script, it's more like a 4-phase script. There are four primary questions, but you will be asking follow-up questions to dig deeper and get more complete answers.

Before prospects get on the phone with you, they fill out an application form so you can pre-qualify them. Then you should have an assistant contact them to set up a 30-minute call.

Once you're on the call, most people will want to open with small talk. That invites them to ramble on and waste time. You don't want that. You want to set yourself up as the one running the call right from the start. So you're going to say:

> Hey, this is Russell and I'm excited to be on the call with you. So here's how these calls work. I'm going to ask you four questions. Depending on how you answer them and how well we get along, we'll decide whether to move forward. Sound fair enough?

They should answer yes, or the call can end right there. You're getting a micro-commitment here, a little yes right at the start. You're also setting the ground rules so you can steer the conversation where you want it to go. Once they agree, it's time to start asking the questions.

THE 4 QUESTIONS CLOSE

Question #1

Imagine you and I were to start working together today. I teach you everything I know and do everything I can to help you get results. Now imagine we're sitting in a coffee shop a year from now. What would have happened in your life, both personally and professionally, for you to feel happy with your progress? What would make you believe that this was the best decision you ever made?

You're trying to get them to describe their external and internal goals here. You want to hear their true desires. If they can't answer this question, you don't want to work with them because you'll never be able to satisfy them. No matter how much you accomplish—and no matter how much they pay you—if they can't articulate their desires, then you won't be able to make them a reality.

Most likely, they'll start by describing external desires. They want to make $10,000 a month. Or they want a boat or a fancy new house in a better school district. They want to lose weight or have a better relationship with their spouse. This is a great start, but you want to dig deeper and get to the internal desires as well. So ask follow-up questions based on their answers.

> Why do you want to make $10,000 a month? Why do you want that fancy new house? What's so important about the school district you're in?

Then they'll start revealing the values and beliefs that are truly important to them. Maybe they want $10,000 a month to prove to their family that they're a good provider. Or maybe they have a favorite charity they want to support in a big way. Maybe they want to be in a good school district because their kids aren't being challenged where they are. Or maybe they are childless and their spouse has given up hope of ever having a family. They are hoping that moving to a good school district will demonstrate that there's still hope.

Do you see how very different those inner desires can be for different people, even though they want the same things? You need to know those inner reasons WHY they want what they want. So keep digging until they reveal those deep emotional connections.

At the end of the day, we all want the same things—respect, inclusion, and purpose. When you dig and dig and eventually they say something that reveals one of these three things, you can stop and move to the next question. They might say, "I just want my father to respect me." Or "I want my life to have a purpose, so I live on when I die." Or "I want to be part of something bigger than myself."

Train yourself to listen carefully for these cues. Then move on to the next question.

Question #2

Clearly, you know what you want. You've painted a really great picture for me. So let me ask you this—why don't you have it yet? What's been standing in your way or holding you back?

Here you're looking for their obstacles and objections. If they don't have what they want yet, there must be a reason. And you need to know whether you can help them with those obstacles or not. If they start blaming other people, you can't help them. Listen for them to say things like "My spouse doesn't support me", or "I tried XYZ program and it didn't work. That guy was useless." If they're blaming other people or outside circumstances for their failures, you really don't want them as a client.

You want people who will take responsibility for their own actions. So listen for some version of "I don't know how." Maybe they say, "I tried XYZ program, but I just didn't understand the finer details. I need to take the time to master the process." The key here is the word *I*. If they talk about themselves a lot, then chances are you can help them. If they don't know how to do something and you can help them, you're going to have a successful relationship.

Next it's time to get them thinking about possibilities.

Question #3

I want you to think about what resources, connections, talents, or skills you have access to that you're not currently utilizing 100%, that we could use to help overcome your obstacles and achieve your goals.

Give them some time to think about it. They might come up with some great answers, or they might come up with something off-the-wall. The point is to get them thinking about the possibilities.

Whatever they come up with is good. Encourage them to keep thinking. Keep asking, "What else? What else?" until they run out of ideas. When they do, you say this:

Okay, so let's review for a minute.

1. It looks like you know exactly what you want. You told me you want _____ because _____.
2. Now you haven't been able to achieve that before primarily because of _____ and _____, right?
3. And last, it looks like you have all these resources you could leverage that you're not leveraging yet, right?

I then ask them, "How much more money do you think you'd make (or how much weight would you lose or how much better would your marriage be) if you were able to eliminate the obstacles and leverage those resources?"

I let them explain to me what will happen.

"Oh man, if I could do that, I'm pretty sure I could make a million dollars (or lose a ton of weight, be so much happier in my marriage)…"

I then transition to the final question.

Question #4
4. So I only have one more question. Do you want me to help you?

Then I stop talking. I don't say another word until they answer. Most of the time, they will say yes. Then all I have to do is say:

Great! Here's how it works. My fee is \$_____. For that money, you get _____. I'm here to help you. I can transfer you over to my assistant to take care of the financial details right now. Would you like to do that?

If they say yes, you're done. Usually the only reason they won't agree at this point is because they don't have the money. If that's the case, you can offer a payment plan.

If you've done a good job with the questions, and they can afford your fee, then you should close most of the people you talk to. Just send them off to your assistant to handle the credit card details, and you're all set. And that's how the 4-Question Close works.

THE PERFECT WEBINAR HACK

As you can see, it takes time to create a Perfect Webinar presentation. Most people spend a week or two creating their first one. And even though I've been using the format for years, I'll often spend a couple of days creating one presentation. While that's really not a long time to create the foundation of millions of dollars in a business, sometimes you don't have that much time.

For example, about two years ago, I was helping a close friend launch a new company that sold automated webinar software. His sales process looked very traditional, and they were getting average sales driving traffic into his funnel. Then he decided to launch an affiliate contest where the winner got $50k.

I thought it would be fun to compete, but I knew the only way I could win was to change how he was selling his product. I had planned on creating a Perfect Webinar, but as the deadline to win the $50k got closer, I ran out of time. I was competing against 100 other affiliates who had been promoting for several weeks, and I was way behind. There were only a few days left before the contest ended.

I was about to give up and just blow it off, but then I had an idea. What if I could quickly create a Perfect Webinar and launch it—in the next 10–15 minutes? Ha! (I had to laugh at myself for a minute. Then I got serious.) I knew I could never pull it off with traditional PowerPoint or Keynote slides. But what if I just wrote out the key components on a whiteboard?

I had no idea if it would work, but it was my only shot. So I started asking myself a lot of the questions I've covered throughout this book. I'm going to run through them quickly for you right now—because that's all I was able to do in the 15 minutes before I went live with this presentation. (NOTE: All these elements could have been much stronger if I'd had more time, but I only had 15 minutes before I went live, so I had to think REALLY fast.)

I want you to see what you can pull together when you use the concepts in this book as guidelines.

Question #1: What's the <u>new opportunity</u> I'm offering?
Answer: Increasing webinar sales using my weekly webinar model

For this product, we were selling automated webinar software, which was nothing new. So I offered them a NEW opportunity to sell more through webinars using my weekly webinar model. This was a new opportunity that most people (at the time) had never heard of.

Question #2: What is the one Big Domino for this offer?
Answer: If I can get them to believe that doing webinars through my model is the only way they can get to 7 figures in the next 12 months, then they have to give me money. So I wrote out this title:

How to Make (at Least) 7 Figures Next Year with THIS Webinar Model

Question #3: What <u>special offer</u> can I create for those who purchase?

Answer: I spent five minutes writing out my stack on a whiteboard, including everything I would give people who purchased through my affiliate link. His software helped people conduct webinars, so I brainstormed things I already had that would complement what he was selling. Here is what my stack looked like:

- What You're Gonna Get...
- The Perfect Webinar Script $497
- The Perfect Webinar Training $9,997
- Video of My Closing LIVE $2,997
- Perfect Webinar Funnel $997
- My Webinar Funnel...Priceless

Total Value: $14,988

Question #4: What is my Epiphany Bridge origin story?

Answer: The story about how I bombed at my first event and Armand Morin taught me how to do the stack

Question #5: What are three <u>false beliefs</u> they have about this new opportunity (the 3 Secrets), and what Epiphany Bridge stories will I tell to break those false belief patterns?

I broke them down like this:

A. What is their #1 false belief about webinars (the vehicle we were putting them into)?

B. What Epiphany Bridge story do I have that got me to believe in webinars?

I knew my epiphany had occurred when I learned the script for how to sell on webinars (which eventually became the Perfect Webinar). So I then wrote on the whiteboard:

Secret #1: It's All About the Script

Then I went into Secret #2.

C. What is their #1 false belief about their personal ability to execute on this vehicle?

D. What Epiphany Bridge story do I have that got me to believe in my abilities?

For me, my big epiphany was understanding how the webinar model worked, and that I could actually do it. So I then wrote on the whiteboard:

Secret #2: Understanding the Model

Finally, I thought about the third secret.

E. What is their #1 false belief or outside force that they think will keep them from success?

F. What Epiphany Bridge story do I have that got me to understand the truth?

For me, my epiphany was understanding that this only works if you do it LIVE every week until it converts to actual results. I then wrote down:

Secret #3: You have to do this LIVE until…

Now those probably weren't the best titles in the world, and I'm sure with a few days of massaging them, I could have made them amazing. But this whole process only took me about 15 minutes.

Then I had to figure out how to promote this message to the most people in the least amount of time. I didn't have time to set up a webinar funnel and get people into a sequence. I needed to start getting sales IMMEDIATELY. So I opened up two of my phones, turned on Facebook Live and Periscope, and clicked "Go Live" on both platforms. Because I already have strong followings in both places, I was live in front of hundreds of people within seconds!

I did the presentation by just talking off the top of my head, sharing my Epiphany Bridge stories, and then going into my stack and close.

Within 26 minutes and 32 seconds, my presentation was done. I had no idea if it was good or bad—it was all so quick. But as I looked at my stats, I saw the sales flooding in.

I was then able to promote those presentations on Facebook and other places for the next three days until the contest was over. During this time, over 100,000 people saw this presentation. We ended up doing over $250,000 in sales and I won the $50k cash prize! Not bad for only 15 minutes of preparation!

And while I thought that was pretty cool, even more exciting was the fact that Brandon and Kaelin Poulin saw what I did and decided to model it. Later that day, they launched a Facebook Live session, and did almost the same thing. They had their stack written down on a whiteboard, and Kaelin wrote her 3 Secrets on paper, which she showed as she was teaching and telling her stories.

Their first try at this process made them over $100,000, and they've gone on to do it each month since. In fact, recently they did over $650,000 from ONE Facebook Live presentation, using the Perfect Webinar script without any PowerPoint slides—just a whiteboard and a few sheets of paper.

As you master the Perfect Webinar script and you get better at telling stories and delivering your offer, you can use it to sell almost any product with just a few minutes notice. The Perfect Webinar is perfect. The only time it doesn't work is when people mess it up by not following what I've laid out in this book. In fact, if you try it and it doesn't work, I can tell you from experience it's probably for one of these reasons:

1. You picked a bad market and no one wants to hear what you have to say.
2. You built an improvement offer and no one wants to buy it.
3. You slipped into teaching mode and didn't create an environment for change.

If you pick a good market, make a new opportunity that is truly irresistible, and then use your presentation to break and rebuild their belief patterns around that new opportunity…it works. I promise!

As you follow what I do online, you'll see me using this script and story process in all sorts of situations, including video sales letters, teleseminars, product launch videos, Google Hangouts, Facebook Live videos, and even in my email sequences.

On the following page is a cheat sheet you can use to structure your Perfect Webinars fast.

PERFECT WEBINAR CHEAT SHEET

Question #1: What's the <u>new opportunity</u> I'm offering?

Question #2: What is the one <u>Big Domino</u> for this offer?

Question #3: What <u>special offer</u> can I create for those who purchase?

Question #4: What is my Epiphany Bridge <u>origin story?</u>

Question #5: What are three <u>false beliefs</u> they have about this new opportunity (the 3 Secrets), and what <u>Epiphany Bridge stories</u> will I tell to break those false belief patterns?

A. False Belief (Vehicle)

B. Epiphany Bridge Story (Vehicle)

C. False Belief (Internal)

D. Epiphany Bridge Story (Internal)

E. False Belief (External)

F. Epiphany Bridge Story (External)

EMAIL EPIPHANY FUNNELS

EPIPHANY SOAP OPERA SEQUENCE

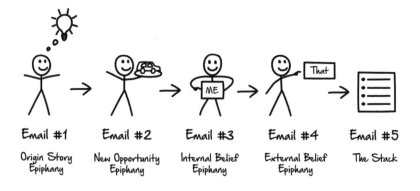

Email #1	Email #2	Email #3	Email #4	Email #5
Origin Story Epiphany	New Opportunity Epiphany	Internal Belief Epiphany	External Belief Epiphany	The Stack

One of my biggest breakthroughs happened when I realized that I could use this Perfect Webinar process in ALL areas of my marketing, including email. In *DotComSecrets*, I talked about a concept I learned from Andre Chaperon called Soap Opera Sequences (SOS), which are the emails you send to someone when they first join your list. He called them soap opera sequences because each email ends with a hook that draws you to the next episode, just like a soap opera does.

For years, I had been using SOS emails with different story structures. (I even shared some in the DotComSecrets book.) But when I started seeing people use the Perfect Webinar in different situations like Facebook Live and video sales letters, I had a thought…I wonder if this would also work as an email sequence? In fact, I wonder if I could do ALL the selling by email, and not even push them into attending a presentation. It seemed so crazy, I figured it just might work. So I took the Perfect Webinar and broke down the four core stories and the stack, added each into an email, and tested it out. The results were…well, they were amazing! So much so that we are now going back and adding them into every funnel we have.

There are a few different ways that we've successfully used this so far. The first was just writing out each story for the emails. The second way was making videos telling each of the stories, and then linking to the video inside of the emails. Honestly the way they receive the story matters less then following the actual story structure that you learned about earlier in this book.

One of the keys to remember in soap opera sequence like this is that each email needs to pull people into the next story in the next email. Think about how good soap operas, reality shows and most shows on TV are able to pull you through the commercial breaks and week to week by getting you excited by what is about to happen, then cutting it off. We do the same thing in these emails, teasing about the next email that's coming so they are anxiously waiting for it.

EPIPHANY PRODUCT LAUNCH FUNNELS

EPIPHANY BRIDGE PRODUCT LAUNCH

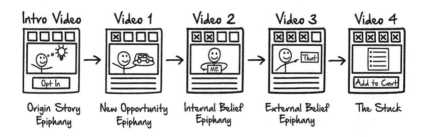

Intro Video	Video 1	Video 2	Video 3	Video 4
Origin Story Epiphany	New Opportunity Epiphany	Internal Belief Epiphany	External Belief Epiphany	The Stack

W hen ClickFunnels was getting close to its one-year anniversary, we wanted to create a new funnel in hopes that we could get some of the same affiliate partners who had promoted our Perfect Webinar in the past to promote again. We knew that many of them would not want to just promote the same webinar to their followers again, so we decided to switch from a webinar to a product launch funnel.

Inside the *DotComSecrets* book, I also shared our product launch funnels, as well as the scripts we've had success with in the past inside of the product launch funnels. But I knew that the messaging and stories in our webinars worked really well, so why not just use them again here? And with that, we basically just recreated the Perfect Webinar and Epiphany Bridge stories inside of the product launch funnel structure.

I recorded an intro video telling my origin story, then had them opt in for the rest of the videos in the sequence. Then video #1 became Secret #1, which told them about the new opportunity. Secret #2 focused on their internal beliefs, and Secret #3 their external beliefs. Then video #4 was just a video of me doing the stack.

It worked amazingly well, and since then I've seen dozens of others create product launch funnel versions of their Perfect Webinars. One of the most powerful ways we've used—and that I've started to see others adopt as well—is after someone comes through your webinar funnel, to send emails to those who didn't show up to the webinar, and have them go through the product launch sequence instead. That way, those who didn't get a chance to consume your message can get it in a different format they may be more likely to watch.

WHAT'S NEXT?

Now that you have created your presentation and the funnels that people will go through to get your message, the next questions I get a lot are "How do I get people into those funnels? What is the fuel that will ignite my following so I can start a mass movement?"

This section will show you how to fill your funnels and mention some other things you can do to jump-start your success as an expert.

FILL YOUR FUNNEL

The million-dollar question everyone asks after they learn about funnels is "How do you actually get people into those funnels?" I had the same question when I got started. In fact, I remember asking a friend who was having a lot of success online at the time, "How do you create traffic?"

He smiled and said, "Russell, you don't need to create traffic, it's already there. People are already online. You just have to figure out how to get those people to leave where they are and come to you instead."

The wheels in my head started spinning. I started thinking about WHERE my dream customers were already congregating. I realized that, in most cases, the people I wanted to serve were already in the market looking for something. And if I could present them with MY new opportunity, I could get them to leave where they were and start following me.

About that same time, I heard about a concept called the "Dream 100" from one of my friends and mentors, Chet Holmes. Early in Chet's career, he worked for Charlie Munger, who you may know was Warren Buffet's partner in Berkshire-Hathaway. Chet sold advertising for one of the company's legal magazines. At the time, they were really struggling. Chet was working with a database of over 2,000 advertisers. He made calls and sent out materials every day. But they were still #16 out of 16 magazines in their industry. Dead last.

Then Chet got smart. He did some research and discovered that out of those 2,000 advertisers, 167 of them were spending 90% of their advertising budgets with his competitors. So he defined those 167 as his best buyers—the ones spending all the money in the industry. Once he figured that out, he stopped marketing to everybody and instead focused his time and efforts on those 167. He sent out direct-mail pieces with lumpy objects in them every two weeks, then he followed up with a few phone calls. Twice a month he'd mail, twice a month he'd call.

Now Chet was known for what he called "PHD"—Pig-Headed Determination. So he just kept going after those same people month after month. Because these were the biggest buyers, they were the hardest people to reach. But he didn't give up. After four months of following this strategy, he got zero response. (Pretty discouraging, right?)

Then in his fourth month, something changed. He landed his first big account—Xerox. It was the biggest advertising buy ever for the company. By the sixth month, he had landed 29 of the 167. And with those 29, Chet doubled the sales over the previous year. They went from #16 to #1 in the industry in just over a year. And he kept doubling sales for the next three years.

Later on in his career, Chet wrote a screenplay and wanted to sell it to a big Hollywood studio. So he followed the same Dream 100 strategy. He researched and found 100 Hollywood producers, actors, directors, and other people who could make his film a reality. He focused on his Dream 100 list and relentlessly pursued these guys. And yes, eventually he did sell his film to one of those big studios.

So what does this have to do with you?

Well, when I first heard Chet explain how the Dream 100 worked, I realized that there were probably 100 people who already had MY dream customers. They had the traffic. I didn't need to create it, I just needed to figure out how to get those people to come and see my new opportunity instead.

The first step in this Dream 100 process was going back to Secret #1. Remember when I created my new niche? We started with the three hot markets (health, wealth, and relationships).

THE 3 MARKETS

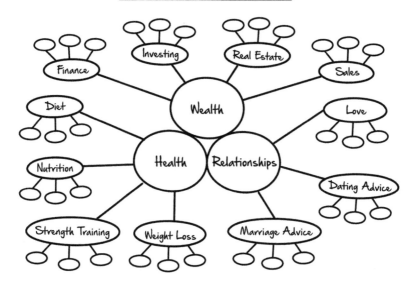

From there, I drilled down into a sub-niche inside of one of those markets. Then within that sub-niche, I created my new opportunity.

I found that the key to the Dream 100 was to step back from my niche and go back up to the submarket level. Inside of that submarket are all the niches where my traffic is already congregating. All I needed to do was figure out WHO was controlling that traffic.

WHERE TO FIND YOUR DREAM 100?

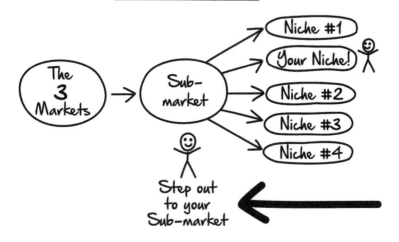

I quickly realized that the people who controlled that traffic were typically one of four types: list owners, bloggers, podcasters, or social media influencers (including YouTube, Instagram, Twitter, Facebook, etc.) I started searching and found list owners with email lists of 20,000 to 200,000 or more of my dream customers! Bloggers and podcasters who had millions of readers and listeners and social media influencers who could drive tens of thousands of clicks to anything they wanted to talk about. I saw their power, so I started to build out my Dream 100 list of these people and companies. Initially, I tried to find 25 list owners in my submarket, 25 bloggers, 25 podcasters, and 25 social media influencers.

List Owners	Bloggers	Podcasts	Social Media
1. _____	1. _____	1. _____	1. _____
2. _____	2. _____	2. _____	2. _____
3. _____	3. _____	3. _____	3. _____
4. _____	4. _____	4. _____	4. _____
5. _____	5. _____	5. _____	5. _____

After I filled out that list, I had the 100 people who already had the attention of those I wanted to serve. Then I put together a plan to infiltrate my Dream 100.

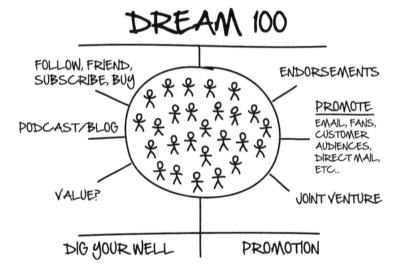

The first goal was to start building relationships with my Dream 100. As Harvey Mackay said, you want to "dig your well before you're thirsty". The WORST time to contact your Dream 100 is the day you need them to promote something for you. The best time to start building relationships is NOW. So when you are ready to ask them to promote you, that relationship will already be there.

Dig Your Well Strategy #1 I started by following them, sending friend requests, subscribing to their emails lists, blogs, and podcasts, and buying their products. I wanted to put them on my radar so I could see what they were doing and get to know who they were before I made my first contact.

There is nothing worse than getting a meeting with an influencer and not knowing who they are, what they're working on, or what's important to them. I've met a lot of people through the years who somehow make it through my gatekeepers, but when they get on the phone, they're so focused on selling me something that we never get past the first few minutes. If you want to build a relationship with your Dream 100, you need to be prepared.

Dig Your Well Strategy #2 After I know who they are and understand what's important to them, I want to give them a platform that helps to promote them, but at the same time gives me the ability to build a relationship with them. My favorite way to do that is to interview them for my podcast or my blog. I can usually get 30–60 minutes to ask them questions and build a relationship during that interview.

When I promote that interview, it helps them as well. Most of my best partners started with me interviewing them and then taking that relationship from the interview into Strategy #3.

Dig Your Well Strategy #3 Now that I have a basic relationship with them, one of the main things I like to ask (and I learned this from Sean Stephenson) is what project they're working on that is most important to them at the moment. After they tell me, I figure out what extra value I can offer to help them reach their goal. And that's it. It's simple, but it's how great business relationships are built. I'm digging my well BEFORE I'm thirsty.

When should you start "digging your well"? You need to start this strategy NOW, no matter where you are in your business today.

After you've spent time digging your well, start looking for ways to leverage these relationships to gain access to their followers. If you have created a truly new opportunity that will serve their audience, then there are lots of ways you can work together. If you've "picked" a niche, then you'll likely be in direct competition with many of your Dream 100. But if you've created your niche—your new opportunity—then you should be complementary to most of them. This makes the promotion process a lot easier.

Promotion Strategy #1 The easiest and best way to work with your Dream 100 is to get them to promote you and your new opportunity to their following. That's my #1 goal. I focus hard on the relationship. And when the time is right, I ask them to promote my webinar. I reach out to my Dream 100 by sending them a physical newsletter and package in the mail every month with information about the special promotions we are running and how they can be part of them. Even though my Dream 100 has grown to nearly 600 people, I still send a package and give them a call every month.

Not everyone on my Dream 100 will promote my products. In fact, many of them I can never even get on the phone. But I consistently market to them, because one YES can put me in front of their audience of hundreds of thousands of people or more! I've had times when one person on my Dream 100 has said yes, and within three months that relationship netted over a million dollars. It's worth consistently building relationships with those people. I would say that about 30% of the traffic into my funnels comes from this strategy.

Promotion Strategy #2 While my main goal is to get my Dream 100 to promote my product, oftentimes they can't or won't, and that's okay. Over the past few years, most of the social networks have opened up their advertising platforms so I can promote to the fans and followers of specific people or companies. For example, I can go to Facebook and show ads to all the Tony Robbins fans (one of my Dream 100). You could go to Twitter and target Ashton Kutcher's followers (if he's in your Dream 100).

So I create specific ads to target the followers of each person on my Dream 100 list. Each network is different and they change frequently, so you'll need to stay on top of the networks you want to use. But if you go to www.FillYourFunnel.com, you can see the most up-to-date training for each network. About 40% of my traffic comes from this strategy.

Promotion Strategy #3 So where does the last 30% come from? About 10% comes from marketing, search engine optimization, and other things we're doing each day, but the last 20% comes from something I learned called "integration marketing" from my first mentor, Mark Joyner. He wrote an awesome book by the same name that shows you how to integrate into the sales flow of your Dream 100.

If you look at the sales path that customers of people on your Dream 100 are going through, you can find places where it would make sense for your products or services to be offered. The idea is to integrate your offers into their natural sales funnel. Can you put one of your products on one of their thank-you pages? Can you put your ad in a PS on their emails? Could you co-create a product that you both promote and both get customers from? How can you integrate into your Dream 100 sales funnels? This way, it's not just one and done, instead you will get a continuous stream of customers. There are thousands of creative ways to integrate with your Dream 100.

There are so many ways to drive traffic and fill your funnels. But ALL my strategies are built on the foundation of the Dream 100. When you understand the strategy behind how and why this works, you can quickly and easily start getting customers into your funnel. Again, the tactics will change. But if you master the Dream 100 strategy, you will always be able to fill your funnels with new people.

CONCLUSION:
YOUR INVITATION

P hew!

I'm sure that right now you're probably feeling like you have been drinking from a fire hose, and I totally understand that. The concepts I've laid out here took me over 10 years to discover from dozens of different mentors and a whole lot of trial and error. I wish I'd had something like this when I got started. I hope that instead of feeling overwhelmed, you'll realize that this is actually a huge shortcut.

I only shared in these pages those things that have been proven to work in my own and our other members' businesses. You can have faith, knowing that you're implementing stuff that has been proven in hundreds of different markets.

The diagrams that I included in each chapter should also help you quickly recall the core messages so you'll be able to reflect on them over and over again and refer to them quickly as you build your cult-ure, create your products, tell your stories, and build your funnels.

If you're wondering where you should start, this is what I'd recommend.

1. Become VERY clear about who you want to serve and what new opportunity you will create.
2. Get results for your beta group. Your results will become the foundation your expert business will grow from.
3. Become a master storyteller. This is the most important skill you can learn.
4. Change the world. Your message has the ability to change people's lives, so use it.

I hope that reading this book has been a great investment of your time. I spent over 18 months writing it and rewriting it because I wanted it to be perfect for you. But no matter how good you make a book, it can never be as good as having me or my team work with you personally on your funnel, stories, and presentation. If you'd like to work more closely with us to develop your expert business, I invite you to attend one of our Funnel Hack-a-Thon events.

During these events, we spend a few days in a small group working together to build your mass movement, create your stories, build your presentation, and launch your funnels. If you'd be interested in coming to our next Funnel Hack-a-Thon, you can get more information at www.FunnelHackAThon.com.

After you apply there, someone on my team will contact you. If you're a good fit, we could be meeting at my office later this month. I'm a big believer that money follows speed. Don't let this opportunity pass you by—let's get your message out to the world.

I also invite you to join our private Facebook group of fellow Funnel Hackers like yourself. You can meet others who are using this process and can share their stories with you. Join us at www.ProjectClickFunnels.com.

Now that we're wrapping up *Expert Secrets*, I want to end where we started. Throughout our lives, we go through different stages. For most of us in this expert space, there was a time when we focused on growth. We studied books, learned and tested things, and became the people we felt we needed to become. We each followed our own path.

And no matter how much time we focused on growth, after a while it got old. We started to wonder, *Is there anything else? There's got to be more.* We get to that stagnation point, because growth is just half of what we need to have true fulfillment in life.

The second half of fulfillment comes from contribution.

I want to congratulate you for taking that next step—moving beyond mere personal growth and deciding to use your life lessons to contribute and help others. I know that as you do that, you'll become more and more fulfilled. This is one of the wonderful benefits of launching an expert-based business and selling products and programs.

Throughout this book, I've talked a lot about conversion rates and how to make the most money from the least amount of ad spend. And that's great. It's important. But what it all comes down to—what matters the most—is not how much money you make. It's how many lives you impact. The money is just a cool way to keep track of what's happening.

Getting people to give you money is also one of the best ways you can hold them accountable to their goals. I struggled with my business for almost two years because I was so scared of investing in myself. I was never able to ask other people to invest in the products and services I created either. It wasn't until I started making financial commitments with different coaches and mentors that I was finally able to become congruent. Because I was investing in myself, I was able to go out and ask others to invest in themselves with my products and services.

I know selling may not be your favorite activity. But when people pay you, it gives them the transformation they need to change their lives. It's a cool cycle that we have a chance to go through—you get to create something, test it out and, if it works, you get paid. The more you focus on that cycle, the more lives you will be able to change.

The Expert Secrets process focuses on one core funnel, the Perfect Webinar—getting you into the habit of producing a live event every single week. Consistency pays! And if you spend any time inside my ClickFunnels or Funnel Hacker communities, you know there are lots of other ways to monetize your knowledge, provide value to your customers, and make money. You can just keep stacking funnel upon funnel based on what your audience needs and wants.

I want to invite you to hang out with me and the other amazing people in my world. Spend time in our Facebook groups, watch our videos, come to our events, and make friends with other people like you. They may be in a different market and have a different message, but they have the same mission. They're trying to change the world in their own little way. That's been my driving force for the last decade, and I just feel so blessed to have a chance to work with entrepreneurs like you who are doing the exact same thing.

With that said, I encourage you to master the skills in this book. Become a master storyteller. Really become the vehicle for change that I know you can be. After you've done that, I encourage you to go deeper. Spend more time with us and figure out how to take your company, your business, and your customers' lives to the next level.

Thanks for spending this time with me. I'll talk to you soon.

Russell Brunson

PS: Remember, you're just one funnel away…

REFERENCES

Abagnale, Frank with Stan Redding. *Catch Me If You Can: The True Story of a Real Fake*. Broadway Books. 2000.

Abraham, Jay. Google Plus. "People are silently begging to be led…" (blog post) November 21, 2011. https://plus.google.com/102305438832315209054/posts/gpHa7BT1D91

"Apple Steve Jobs—The Crazy Ones (Original Post)". YouTube. 1997. https://www.youtube.com/watch?v=8rwsuXHA7RA

The Bible (King James Version). Proverbs 29:18.

The Book of Mormon. Ed. The Church of Jesus Christ of Latter-day Saints. Salt Lake City: The Church of Jesus Christ of Latter-day Saints, 2006. Alma 46:10-14

Brunson, Russell. *DotCom Secrets: The Underground Playbook for Growing Your Company Online*. Morgan James Publishing. 2015.

Churchill, Winston. The Imaginative Conservative. "A Man's Finest Hour" (quote) http://www.theimaginativeconservative.org/2011/08/quote-of-day-mans-finest-hour.html

Cruise, Tom. *Jerry Maguire*. DVD. Directed by Cameron Crowe. Columbia TriStar Home Video, 1997.

Dwinell, Mason. *Eat the Sun*. Directed by Peter Sorcher. Amazon Video, 2011.

Fladlien, Jason. *Pitch Webinar Secrets 2.0*. Pages 4-7 and 30-46. http://webinarpitchsecrets.com. 2013.

Jones, Felicity. *Rogue One: A Star Wars Story*. Directed by Gareth Edwards. Walt Disney Studios Motion Pictures, 2016.

Kelly, Kevin. The Technium. "1,000 True Fans" (article). March 4, 2008. http://kk.org/thetechnium/1000-true-fans/

Kim, W. Chan and Renée Mauborgne. *Blue Ocean Strategy*. Harvard Business Review Press. 2005.

Gibson, Mel. *Braveheart*. DVD. Directed by Mel Gibson. Paramount Home Video, 2002.

Hauge, Michael and Christopher Vogler. *The Hero's 2 Journeys*. Audio CD. Writer's AudioShop. 2003.

Hoffer, Eric. *The True Believer: Thoughts on the Nature of Mass Movements*. Harper Perennial Modern Classics. 2010.

Holmes, Chet. *The Ultimate Sales Machine: Turbocharge Your Business with Relentless Focus on 12 Key Strategies*. Portfolio. 2007.

Jobs, Steve. "Apple Music Event 2001-The First Ever iPod." YouTube. https://www.youtube.com/watch?v=kN0SVBCJqLs

Joyner, Mark. *Integration Marketing Integration Marketing: How Small Businesses Become Big Businesses—and Big Businesses Become Empires*. Wiley. 2009.

Klaver, Kim. *If My Product's So Great, How Come I Can't Sell It?* Kim Klaver. 2004.

McEvoy, James and Michael Fassbender. *X-Men: First Class*. DVD. Directed by Matthew Vaughn. 20th Century Fox Home Entertainment, 2011.

Sheidies, Nick. Incomediary.com. "11 Life-Changing Business Lessons from Zig Ziglar" (article). http://www.incomediary.com/zig-ziglar-life-changingbusiness-lessons

Sullivan, Dan. *The Dan Sullivan Question*. The Strategic Coach, Inc. 2009.

Warren, Blair. *The One Sentence Persuasion Course: 27 Words to Make the World Do Your Bidding*. Blair Warren. 2013.

Wilson, Owen. *Cars*. DVD. Directed by John Lasseter. Buena Vista Home Entertainment, 2006.

Morgan James
Speakers Group

🖋 www.TheMorganJamesSpeakersGroup.com

We connect Morgan James published authors with live and online events and audiences whom will benefit from their expertise.